VISITING
HEAVEN

VISITING HEAVEN

HEAVENLY KEYS TO A
LIFE WITHOUT LIMITATIONS

CAPTAIN DALE BLACK

DESTINY IMAGE® PUBLISHERS, INC.
P.O. Box 310, Shippensburg, PA 17257-0310
"Publishing cutting-edge prophetic resources to supernaturally empower the body of Christ"

This book and all other Destiny Image and Destiny Image Fiction books are available at Christian bookstores and distributors worldwide.

For more information on foreign distributors, call 717-532-3040.

Reach us on the Internet: www.destinyimage.com.

ISBN 13 TP: 978-0-7684-6334-7
ISBN 13 eBook: 978-0-7684-6335-4
ISBN 13 HC: 978-0-7684-6337-8
ISBN 13 LP: 978-0-7684-6336-1

For Worldwide Distribution.
1 2 3 4 5 6 7 8 / 27 26 25 24 23

DEDICATION

This book is dedicated to the founder and pastor of the Household of Faith Church in Benton, Arkansas, Pastor Bob Joyce. His Bible teaching is loving, mature, relevant, and profoundly anointed with the Holy Spirit!

Pastor Bob is being used of God in modern times, much like the apostle Paul was in his day. Every word he speaks, every song he sings and plays, exudes the attributes of a man who has died to self and lives solely to glorify the Lord Jesus.

I never thought I would live to see a pastor conduct himself with simultaneous confidence and humility, strength and meekness. But then there is Pastor Joyce. It is evident to me that God prepared this leader his entire life to become one of God's 5-Star Generals of the Faithful Remnant in these last days.

Visiting Heaven is dedicated to Pastor Bob Joyce, purified by fire, leading by example, for such a time as this.

ACKNOWLEDGMENTS

The author wishes to recognize and thank the following people for their valuable contributions to *Visiting Heaven: Heavenly Keys to a Life Without Limitations.*

Shaun Tabatt, Publishing Executive with Destiny Image—the man who gets the impossible accomplished, who has been the perfect liaison, a superb encourager, and genuine pleasure to work with throughout the writing and publishing process.

Paula Black—for her masterful and professional writing and editing expertise, and for her personal support and wise counsel for this project.

Karen Burkett Weigand with Christian Editing and Design—for her exceptional editing and polishing skills, as well as her priceless creative contributions.

Georgia Collett—for her excellent command of the English language, and her quality writing and editing assistance with the stories.

Jerry Payne—for his impeccable writing insights and intellectual input.

Randy Kay—for his personal encouragement and ministerial support, and for graciously contributing the well-written foreword.

CONTENTS

FOREWORD

By Randy Kay

When Dale Black first shared with me his story about Heaven, I became instantly mesmerized, not only because this true story offers a compelling account, but it also resonated with me in a very personal way. I too died and met Jesus in Heaven.

Over the course of years now, I have interviewed numerous individuals who have died and entered the afterlife, many of whom, including Dale, have been on our television show, vodcasts, and afterlife conferences. I think that I have now interviewed the most Christ-honoring afterlife accounts on social media.

What uniquely struck me about Dale's account was an instant respect for this amazing man. I also related with his experience as being real and authentic. Both in my spirit and through my own heavenly journey, I can confirm that Dale's story and descriptions are without a doubt true and foretelling of what believers in Jesus as their Lord and Savior can expect after they leave this world.

Within *Visiting Heaven: Heavenly Keys to a Life Without Limitations.*, Dale brilliantly combines glued-to-the-page storytelling and captivating revelations of Heaven (and hell) in an entertaining and transforming narrative. Some of what Dale Black shares in this book are fresh accounts that, to my knowledge, have not previously been shared publicly. For example, I, like many others, knew that Capt. Dale Black operated as a successful pilot, and some know that God miraculously restored his sight to qualify as a pilot, but did you know that in the emergency room after a fatal plane crash, Dale and his copilot who died, struggled with terrifying evil forces? Did you know about the angelic guides that accompanied Dale on his journey and the singular insights these spiritual beings and God revealed to Dale? How about the city of Heaven that Dale viewed and describes in breathtaking detail? These and other deep insights are sure to build your faith and wisdom.

As a fellow sojourner in Heaven and a researcher of afterlife experiences, I can testify that Dale's descriptions are not only accurate, but his writings also combine Dale's heavenly insights with a practical application of how we can live more abundantly in this life. For example, Dale explains that his experience has "sown the promise [of God] in [his] heart." He references this pearl of wisdom to persevere for the lost "until he is found."

Anyone who glimpses Heaven can appreciate the grander purpose God intends for us, but it takes a gifted teacher like Dale to impart a revelation to the reader so that he or she can live more faithfully as *"unto the Lord,"* as it says in Colossians 3:23.

Yes, Captain Dale Black offers some seasoned descriptions of his worldwide flight journeys and a breathtaking journey of flying within the heavenlies, but the reader's takeaway should be what Heaven teaches us. Dale learned that "communication was heart to heart, not through the ears and mind." Indeed, communication in Heaven is heart to heart, as it should be in this world. Dale explains some of these heart-to-heart meetings during his missionary journeys. I think it is important to hear how an emissary from Heaven like Dale, brings Heaven's impartation through his earthly service to God in contrast to how we are commonly trained to behave in this world.

Heaven changes you. It colors every action on earth with the flavor of God's mission in the moments and events of life. Ultimately in this book, Dale brings Heaven to the reader's world, and that inevitably will change you, mold you into the person God wants you to be to faithfully serve out the purpose God has ordained for you.

Visiting Heaven will take off on literal "runways" to Russia, Africa, and ultimately to Heaven, and it will bring you to a personal engagement with Dale and his wonderful wife, Paula. After Dale's sojourn in Heaven, he and his wife struggled through a near fatal battle with cancer, and they co-authored an uplifting book titled *Life, Cancer and God: Healing Your Body, Soul, & Spirit*. Of course, Captain Dale Black also wrote the best-selling book *Flight to Heaven*. I love both books, and I think this newest book from Dale serves as the culmination of so many life lessons mixed with his breakthrough experience in Heaven.

I have found that it takes many years for afterlife survivors to fully assimilate the lessons learned from their afterlife encounters. It takes the rest of their lifetimes after returning from Heaven to allow the Holy Spirit to illuminate the reasons why God returned them to this world. Dale has discovered those answers.

Most of us who have been to Heaven do not want to return to this broken world, but invariably God returns His beloved from Heaven to this world to fulfill a profound purpose. It may sound trite to say that this general purpose is to convey the love of God to a fallen world, but the truth is that few, in my experience, are equipped with the narrative-writing skill to cut through the scintillation of explaining Paradise to convey a deeper meaning to it all. Dale Black is one of those rare individuals who can tell a story entertainingly while embedding it with a richness that leads to true revelation—and that leads to a transformation of the heart.

On a personal note, Dale is a special friend to me because we both have seen into the heart of God, and that brings us together in both understanding and appreciation in a way that, quite frankly, can only be fully appreciated by those who have experienced Heaven in the afterlife. We also tend to reflect the raw emotion that comes from being in the presence of God, and I find a special *koinonia* with my friend because of our kindred experiences. The good news is, you will experience that same wonder after you depart this life; and you can catch a glimpse of it in this book.

Also, Dale is one of those Christian leaders who stands on the Rock (Jesus) so faithfully, that he can speak prophetically about God's plans without being at the mercy of the shifting nature of this world. He is truly a man of integrity and honor and faithfulness and intellect and wisdom and discernment. He is God's man.

You need to read or hear what Dale says because he speaks as a messenger of truth with heavenly insight. I am so honored to write the foreword of a book that I know will transform lives. I pray a blessing over you as you escape into the pages of *Visiting Heaven*.

With appreciation and love,

RANDY KAY
Founder, Randy Kay Ministries
Author, *Revelations from Heaven* and *Dying to Meet Jesus*
Producer and host of the television show and vodcast,
Heaven Encounters on ISN and METV and the
Randy Kay YouTube Channel

PROLOGUE

On July 18, 1969, I boarded a commuter airplane with two other pilots. I was just nineteen—a brash young pilot in flight training. Moments later, my life would be forever altered. Just after takeoff, we violently and ironically, crashed into a cemetery's seven-story-high air mausoleum dedicated to famous pilots.

I was the only survivor.

Following this fatal airplane crash and during three days in a coma, I took an uncharted visit to Heaven. This presented its own problem. I'm trained as an engineer. I was raised in a business world where logic ruled. An experience of the heart was well outside my comfort zone. I had no desire to operate in the realm of the unprovable.

This line of thinking was confirmed by my grandfather when I shared with him the story of my heavenly journey immediately after my memory returned. He cautioned me about telling others. "Dale, if your experience really is sacred, then why not keep it to yourself? Instead of telling others about it, why not live your life in a way that reflects your journey to Heaven? Live what you believe you saw. Live what you believe you heard and learned. Dale, your life's actions might speak louder than your words."

And then, not long after the crash, I attended a church service where a man claimed to have died, visited Heaven, and came back to life. I found the service more sensational than sacred. The very essence of Heaven is God and His glory, yet the people seemed more interested in the man with his sensational story than the One who created it all and whom Heaven is all about. My decision not to discuss my journey with anyone was further solidified, and I made a solemn vow to myself and to God not to share my experience with anyone *unless and until* God made it crystal-clear to do so.

As time went on, another reason for remaining silent about Heaven presented itself. Perhaps it became the main reason: Have I really lived as a reflection of Heaven? At various times in my life, I have been truly disappointed in myself. Since I believe I have clearly seen Heaven and was so dramatically changed by the experience, why did I fail again and again to be the man I believed God wanted me to be? Why did I often fall short of being the reflection of what I had seen and heard and learned? It would take me decades to come to grips with the fact that, notwithstanding my glimpse into the eternal, I am human and a very flawed human at that.

Whereas I had at one time determined to leave the story only for my children and grandkids, it has become clear that God intended for me to share it more broadly. Like Jonah in the Bible, I have resisted. I have wrestled fiercely against the idea and have lost many nights of sleep. However, I am fully persuaded that God has instructed me to make my entire heavenly journey public. In my heart, I did fulfill my vow. For over forty years, I lived my experience rather than talked about it. I sure tried anyway.

After having flown and worked and ministered for over four decades before telling this story, I've raised a family who learned about a loving God and much about His Word. I completed my vocational assignments. Now past retirement age, I believe I have been instructed by the Lord to revisit my journey to Heaven and share the entire story. You may find that believable, or you may not. Just as you may or may not find the story itself believable. This is perfectly understandable. After all, I did have massive head injuries from the crash. I was on pain medication. It would be easy and convenient to imagine these as reasons for the story I am about to relate.

And yet what I experienced was so real to me that my entire life and the way I lived it changed completely and permanently. Yes, sometimes the logical engineer in me comes out and challenges what my mind remembers, but in all these years, my heart has never questioned. My heart has always believed. And my heart always wins.

I suppose it's a bit like being in love. Does love always make sense? Of course not. But that doesn't mean it doesn't change you. For those of you who have experienced the new birth, perhaps it can be likened to salvation. You wonder sometimes intellectually if you're really saved. If so, how can you continue being so human, so flawed? And yet you know, in your heart, that everything changed when you surrendered your life to Jesus Christ.

For me, on that July day in 1969, my life was turned upside down. My priorities were turned inside out. My focus turned toward eternity rather than the trappings of this world. Since then, I volunteered on almost a thousand ministry flights to more than fifty countries—helping to build churches, orphanages, and medical clinics. I've trained and led teams of lay ministers and medical personnel to help the needy worldwide at my own expense. Every major decision I have made—including giving up an airline career, selling our personal multimillion-dollar aviation business, and donating those funds into the ministry—was a direct result of my journey to Heaven.

Those who have known me might now well understand why I've seemed like a bit of a misfit, why my life has often followed an offbeat, even illogical path.

If my experience was merely a dream, why has it continued wielding its powerful influence for over half a century? Why wouldn't it simply fade away? Why, for just a dream, would one sacrifice reputation, career, financial security, and more? Why would one continue making major life choices that result in great personal cost?

That brings us to this point. If I do my job correctly, what you'll gain in the following pages will be a better and clearer understanding of who God is. You'll learn about my flight to Heaven, about how and why Heaven miraculously transformed me. Not only that, but you'll also better understand how you can successfully interact with the loving God who created you. Not so incidentally, you will also know how you, too, can prepare for Heaven. Heaven *is* real. And the God of the Bible is who this earth-life is all about.

> *Most assuredly, I say to you, he who hears My word and believes in Him who sent Me has everlasting life, and shall not come into judgment, but has passed from death into life* (John 5:24).

Even if you remain unbelieving of what I saw, heard, and learned, you just might come to believe that *something* changed me. And perhaps there is inspiration in that.

Sharing such a personal and revolutionary experience as I do in this book is challenging. I would also like to give a word of caution. A testimony is a person's personal story of what happened to them. It cannot, nor should it ever, supersede God's Word, which is the absolute truth and the final authority.

Thank you for reading. Settle in for the amazing trip we are about to embark upon. Though I would not ask you to disengage your mind, I would like to ask you to read with an open heart. If you'll do that, I think you'll be wonderfully surprised at what God has stored up for you.

CHAPTER 1

THE LAST FLIGHT

It was an especially gorgeous night to fly. Clear skies, cool temperatures, and visibility in excess of fifty miles. After departing Omaha, Nebraska, in the Boeing 727 narrow-body trijet with 139 passengers plus a crew of six, we were on schedule toward Los Angeles International Airport (LAX). This was the last leg of a four-day trip.

The first officer spoke into his headset: "Roger, direct Denver as filed, maintain flight level three four zero. One thirty-three point six five, TWA four fourteen."

To me, being part of the flight crew of a major US airline was nothing short of a miracle. You see, more than ten years earlier I had been a passenger and only survivor of a horrific and ironic airplane crash that the National Transportation Safety Board (NTSB) had declared "non-survivable."

At the scene of the crash site, paramedics had resuscitated my lifeless body—at least temporarily. Once at the hospital, I remained in a coma for three days. During this time, I visited Heaven. On the morning of the fourth day, I awoke forever changed with a profound understanding of things I had never learned on earth. There was also an unmistakable call of God on my life. How could I go back to living a "normal" life with all that had occurred?

Sitting in the cockpit, I reflected on that traumatic event and the aftermath. My injuries were so massive—the medical team was clear—I would never fly again because I'd never be able to walk again or use my left arm or see from my right eye. And those were just a few of my injuries. Yet after a decade of rehabilitation and retraining, here I was, flying for Trans World Airlines (TWA). That was indeed miraculous!

While flying for the airlines, I also ran my own aviation business. Along with my wife, Paula, I had started a jet pilot training, jet charter, and jet sales corporation in Southern California. Our clients were Hollywood film producers, movie stars, politicians, well-known musicians, and large company CEOs. God abundantly blessed us through our business.

At the same time, Paula and I were raising two growing kids and volunteering as youth ministers at church. We were more than busy, but our lives were entirely fulfilling.

As an offering to the Lord for all He had done to restore my life, Paula and I donated flight services, aircraft, and our time and energy to ministry outreach and various humanitarian needs. With God's help, we provided medical and dental support, food, clothing, as well as Bibles and gospel tracts to the needy in many countries. God also made a way for us to build several churches and an orphanage.

A special highlight was spending two summers ministering to the Aguaruna tribe in the jungles of northern Peru alongside medical missionary Dr. Larry Garman. There, God had us build a medical clinic, and we helped provide spiritual and nutritional training to the indigenous people. Most importantly, the simple gospel message of Jesus was shared anywhere and everywhere.

Whatever God blessed us with, we were honored to use to bless others. As a result, millions heard the gospel message and tens of thousands became followers of Jesus Christ.

I was jarred out of my reminiscing by a sound at the cockpit door. *Knock. Knock… Knock.*

Someone in the cabin crew was requesting access with the secret knock that flight crew use to let those in the cockpit know it's "friendly." Swinging the door open, I went back to my duties.

"Hello, gentlemen." Suzanne, the head flight attendant, was checking in. "Captain, we're about to begin meal service. Any turbulence or cautions I should know about?"

I gave Suzanne the update, and as she turned to leave the cockpit, she slowed just enough to slap me on the shoulder and playfully push the back of my head as she walked out the door. You see, Suzanne and I grew up together. We were dear friends since the sixth grade, and we both graduated from Western High School in Anaheim, California. Strangely, we found ourselves working for Howard Hughes's pet company—TWA.

I loved this job—not only for the challenge of flying 209,000 pounds of machinery at over 500 mph through thin air, but also for the comradery of a company of employees striving for aviation excellence.

Ahead and slightly to our right, the brilliant and stunning lights of Las Vegas, Nevada, became visible. Especially on a clear night, there's nothing quite like those lights. From a high altitude, the city, which is surrounded by a desert of black nothingness, appears as an oasis. Millions of bright and colorful lights are compressed into a concentrated area, forming a colorfully lit city in its center.

Astronauts on the International Space Station (ISS) observe and photograph numerous metropolitan areas over the planet. The Vegas Strip, with its brightly lit hotels and casinos, is reputed to be the brightest concentration of light on earth.

Again, my mind wandered back to my visit to Heaven. The lights of Las Vegas pale in comparison with the unimaginable beauty of the light there. Heaven's light comes from a singular source, yet the entire city is bathed in an opaque whiteness that is more intense than the sun but doesn't hurt a person's eyes when gazing into it. Every color ever created exists in Heaven's dazzling light. As wonderful as the beauties of earth are, they are at best a weak imitation of the majesty of Heaven. That eternal image of the golden city of Heaven is forever embedded in my heart and mind.

Flying level at 34,000 feet, we passed Las Vegas and reduced our speed to 460 mph as we began a gradual descent into LAX. I scanned the dials and adjusted the overhead rheostat light used to illuminate my approach descent checklist.

Suddenly, from just behind my head, I heard quiet yet powerful words: "Dale, this is your last flight."

The voice startled me. I knew I had locked the cockpit door! I quickly turned my head to see who was behind me. No one was there. I glanced toward the other pilots as the possible source, but they were busily preparing for approach and landing. Besides, they were in front of me, not behind me.

Who said that? I reached over to feel the door latch with my fingers, verifying the door was indeed closed and locked. My mind was spinning. Cupping my hand around my mouth, I whispered, "God…was that You?" I waited, listening intently. Nothing.

Struggling to concentrate, I forced my attention back to the descending aircraft. As I was setting the pressurization controls for the destination airport, there it was again.

"Dale, this is your last flight…for TWA." That same voice! Just behind me. I spun around. Again, no one was there.

Now there was no doubt who had spoken. It was the familiar still, small voice of God. He had spoken to my heart. However, this time I heard every word so distinctly it was as if I were hearing with both my ears and my heart.

I was reminded of Samuel in the Bible when God spoke to him as a young man. Samuel thought a person was calling him until he realized it was God. That night in the Boeing 727 was just such an occasion.

My thoughts raced, trying to evaluate what was happening. *Why would God say those words?* He had miraculously restored everything I had lost in the crash. It was a testimony of God's power and my faith that I was flying for one of the world's premier airlines after all the injuries and rehabilitation I had been through.

Why would He say this was my last flight for TWA? That's crazy. After answering my prayers and giving me my vocational dreams, why would He ask me to give them up? It made no sense.

It would take years to fully understand what actually happened that night. But, yes, that was my last flight. Not my last flight as a pilot. But it was my last flight with TWA. God had other plans for my life, and as you read further, you will learn about the astonishing ramifications of the words spoken in the cockpit that night.

First, I must take you back to when everything changed. Back to the time when my life was turned upside down by an airplane crash and a visit to Heaven. Only then will you understand how visiting Heaven taught me how to live a life without limits.

But this book isn't just about my story. It's also about you. Because you, too, can learn to live a life without limits. Are you ready?

Let's go back to the beginning.

JULY 18, 1969—HOLLYWOOD-BURBANK, CALIFORNIA

Early in the morning on July 18, 1969, I boarded a commuter airplane with two other pilots. I was just nineteen—a brash young pilot in flight training. I settled into the right seat to fly as copilot. Gene, whom I was meeting for the first time, would fly in the left seat. And Chuck Burns, the pilot in charge, would sit on a temporary third seat between and slightly behind the two cockpit chairs.

Chuck was my mentor. He had taken me under his wing to help me reach my dream of becoming a commercial airline pilot. I handled the tasks Chuck didn't want to do—like loading the cargo and pre-flighting the aircraft—so I could build flight hours. Chuck was the guy I wanted to be. I not only looked up to him, but we had also become great friends.

The sun was just coming up as the engines roared to life. It was a beautiful, clear day. A perfect day for flying. As our airplane began to taxi, Chuck and I both noticed that Gene was shaky on the controls. Chuck abruptly tapped me on the shoulder and motioned for us to change places. I was disappointed not to be in the cockpit where I could log flight time, but without hesitation, I unbuckled and climbed into the jump seat so Chuck could take the right seat. The aircraft raced down the runway and lifted into the air.

Moments later we became newspaper headlines. Just after takeoff, we violently crashed into a concrete and marble seven-story-high mausoleum, which ironically had been erected in memory of famous and deceased aviators. It is called the Portal of the Folded Wings Shrine to Aviation and stands in the middle of Valhalla Memorial Park Cemetery.

The twin-engine Piper Navajo struck the mausoleum five feet from the top of its brightly tiled dome. The report from the NTSB said we collided at an official impact speed of 135 miles per hour. On impact, our airplane shattered into thousands of pieces, sending all three of us slamming head-on into the solid building. We were then catapulted into a free fall, resulting in a bone-crushing impact with the ground seven stories below.

Valhalla Memorial Cemetery Portal of the
Folded Wings Shrine to Aviation (crash site)

CHAPTER 2

HEAVEN IS...

Eye has not seen, nor ear heard, nor have entered into the heart of man the things which God has prepared for those who love Him.
— 1 Corinthians 2:9

When someone learns that I survived a fatal airplane crash and subsequently journeyed to Heaven and back, they often ask me to share something of what I experienced. You may be surprised to learn that my immediate response is a general pushback—a reluctance to talk about Heaven's treasures. I've learned that there is a massive gap between what most people want to hear and what I have been willing to reveal.

You see, Heaven is precious and sacred to me. The descriptions of what I saw and heard often seem trivial in comparison to deeper and more central truths of what Heaven is about. The most profound aspects of Heaven are not what I saw and heard but what I learned. What I came to understand about God is why my life was so transformed. Though I will share those things I saw and heard, you may be surprised at the other aspects of Heaven that I am going to include.

For example, when I arrived in Heaven, almost immediately I noticed the complete absence of pride.

God opposes the proud but gives grace to the humble (James 4:6 ESV).

There is no pretense or selfishness. Heaven is not primarily about you or me or what we get. Heaven is all about God. When anyone gets even a glimpse of the Heaven that God created, earthly pride is vaporized. It's no wonder that the Bible tells us *"Moses was very humble, more than all men who were on the face of the earth"* (Numbers 12:3). Why was he the most humble? The answer's clear. He had seen God.

When you compare the awesomeness of God to our puny lives, pride becomes irrelevant and foolish. As a Christian, everything truly good we have ever done, or will ever do, is because of God's unmerited love and His power in us. Glory is not ours to take.

That explains the Scripture in Revelation 4:10 that describes the twenty-four elders casting their crowns at the Lord's feet. For every reward we receive in Heaven, God's grace and power are the reason. There is nothing any of us can take glory for or be prideful about. It's an amazing and wonderful thing to experience a community where every being is giving glory where glory is due—to God alone. This singular focus creates great joy and gratefulness in Heaven and connects us together as a unified community.

Another aspect of Heaven is the blood. We learn that, on earth, the life of the flesh is in the blood. In fact, in this world, God accepts the shed blood of His Son as atonement for sin. Likewise, in Heaven, shed blood is the essence of what binds everyone together. Talk about perfect love and unity. The blood of Jesus was shed for the forgiveness of sin. The cross is still a central focus in Heaven because it represents how each of us entered such a perfect place.

For the life of the flesh is in the blood, and I have given it to you upon the altar to make atonement for your souls; for it is the blood that makes atonement for the soul (Leviticus 17:11).

You see, it's because of Christ's blood that every individual on earth has the opportunity to become a child of God. No one can *earn* the gift of salvation. It can't be purchased or traded or negotiated. It is because of the blood of the Lamb—shed for you and for me—that we can enter Heaven. So how can pride exist when all one does to gain entrance into Heaven is to believe and receive a free gift?

For by grace you have been saved through faith, and that not of yourselves; it is the gift of God, not of works, lest anyone should boast (Ephesians 2:8-9).

The deeper truths of these things are now embedded in my heart and have profoundly impacted me at my core.

Now do you see what I mean? I've just tried to describe two aspects of Heaven—pride and the blood. Neither can be seen, but both are attributes of Heaven just as holiness and unconditional love are. These are only a few of the qualities I discovered on my journey. These things and more changed me and continue to ripple throughout my life to this day.

At this time of my life, I feel compelled by the Lord to share what I have learned about Heaven. I'll try my best to describe the visual and audio splendors as well as the revelations that I came to understand—all for the purpose of helping you learn more about the God who loves you.

Since there are not enough words in the English language, nor adequate descriptions in any language, to accurately convey the wonders of Heaven, let me start with something easier to describe—the part of the journey that occurred before I went inside the city. When I pause to remember, I am still awed by the majesty.

HEAVEN'S COUNTRYSIDE

The countryside surrounding the wall on the outskirts of the city of Heaven is magnificent beyond words. There seems to be no limit to the natural wonders God created for our sheer enjoyment. For example, thick living forests, vibrantly colorful gardens, crystal-clear lakes, all types of animals, and majestic mountains can be seen throughout. The grasses of Heaven alone took my breath away—like a living carpet of lush green velvet. Never had I imagined witnessing such splendor, such richness, such color and life.

It's so interesting to me how even the seemingly insignificant aspects of Heaven have had a residual effect on my earth life in sometimes crazy ways. Take the grass, for example. Maybe because there was so much of it and I experienced it up close much of the time I was there, it made a lasting impact. I stopped and took note that each blade had visible life in it.

Wherever I stepped, the grass would slowly rise back up and look as if nothing had disturbed it. Each blade was the perfect height with a perfect point at its top, natural in that it was not mowed, but nothing was overgrown. All of Heaven looked perfectly designed, manicured, and maintained, yet I never saw anyone mowing or edging. And none of the grass ever died. It seemed to me that there was more life in a single blade of grass than in all the plant life I'd witnessed on earth.

You may find it interesting that years after my physical recovery from the crash, I became trained as a golf course greens consultant. I sold landscape materials to golf course greens keepers to help them achieve the "perfect" putting greens. I still take notice when I see a meadow or golf course that's a vibrant green. It seems I can't help but point it out to whoever is with me. A perfect green or great looking fairway still offers me a subdued reflection of the Heaven I long for. And even though the grass on earth pales in comparison, it does conjure up the memories of perfection that have stayed with me ever since.

I'm not much of a plant or flower kind of guy on earth, that's for sure. But when I eventually went inside the city, I saw people planting flowers and nurturing plants, apparently for the sheer enjoyment it brought them. I couldn't help but notice that the living foliage was so perfect it looked unusual, at least at first. There were no fallen or dead leaves in the soil, no sign of decay. It seemed from my vantage point that any time anyone touched a plant, there was an automatic emitting of increased light, along with a slight melodic vibration. As new flowers were placed, or existing plants were rearranged, the display of beauty was always enhanced. What appeared perfect before became even more breathtaking by the touch of the gardener.

Let the heavens rejoice, and let the earth be glad; let the sea roar, and all its fullness; let the field be joyful, and all that is in it. Then all the trees of the woods will rejoice before the Lord (Psalm 96:11-12).

My natural curiosity, a characteristic that often got me into trouble on earth, propelled me once again. This helped me learn some rich lessons about life in Heaven. I reached down, desiring to touch the grass, intensely intrigued. I allowed one fingertip to lightly touch a single blade. Small micro tornadoes of light on the blade the moment I contacted it. It startled me a bit, so I pulled my hand back. But since there was no pain and as I was still driven to explore, I used several fingers to touch several blades. It happened again. Tiny swirls of life moved in concentric circles, the result of my simple touch.

The description of what I believe happened still seems inadequate. The little gently whirling circles represent to me that there is a symbiotic relationship between the people of Heaven and all the plant life there. I'm confident that this occurs because of the common life source. It is the life of God that is in both. God is the life in the plants. He is also the life of the eternal beings—the people in Heaven. There is life in all things, and that life responds to the unity created through our touch.

Since my heavenly journey, my perspective on all nature on earth has changed. Every plant on earth is a descendent of God's original, perfect creation. When God created earth, the plants, animals, and all things, He said, *"It is good."* There was no sin and no decay at the time of creation—much like what has always existed in Heaven. In the beginning, nothing died on earth. But since the rebellion and fall of man, the whole earth became corrupted. All of nature suffered due to man's original sin.

> *The creation itself also will be delivered from the bondage of corruption into the glorious liberty of the*

children of God. For we know that the whole creation
groans and labors with birth pangs together until now
(Romans 8:21-22).

There was something else about the grass I should tell you. As I've already mentioned, in Heaven, every plant, down to each lovely blade of grass, receives its life from God. But I should add that its needs are perfectly met by the Creator. Each flower and each plant vibrates with melodies, glorifying God continually, reflecting His life through its very existence. In turn, each organism gives a form of worship to God in a manner unique to its own kind.

It still amazes me when I think about God's life being *in* everything. And in Heaven that life is everywhere. It's God's life. Every living being or life form in Heaven is connected by this life and is infused with a kind of energy. This energy is a byproduct of this life that is in everyone and everything. And I think this is the most wonderful part: The power in it—the force of it all—is love.

THE LIGHT OF HEAVEN

Certain parts of Heaven are so different from earthly things that mere words are simply unavailable. Describing light and how light works, is a good example. Earth light comes from our sun and from manmade illumination. In Heaven, all light comes from one source. Everyone in Heaven knows the source of the light. I knew it immediately without needing anyone to tell me. There was no doubt. None whatsoever. God is the light. It's not right to say that God was "in" the light. No. It's also not correct to say the light "came from" God. God *is* the light. God was and is and forever will be the Light. I realize that from earth's vantage point you probably wonder, "What difference does that make?" But trust me. In Heaven, it makes all the difference.

> *This then is the message which we have heard of him, and declare unto you, that God is light, and in him is no darkness at all* (1 John 1:5 KJV).

There's more. Light doesn't shine *on* things in Heaven. It shines *through* everything. There is also life and energy in the light. The light is brilliant—brighter than the sun—yet it didn't burn my eyes or make me want to shield myself from it. In fact, just the opposite was true. The light drew me in. I wanted to get closer to its source. It was warm and inviting—loving. Inside the light are life and love. It's like the three qualities of light are one—Light, Life, and Love.

This light of love and life flows through everything—touching and ministering to every part. The three qualities of light are an extension of the source of Heaven, flowing through the wall, through the plants, and even through me, continuously infusing me with energy and life and bathing my soul in love.

The warm and brilliant light washed through the beautiful gate unimpeded. If you can picture in your mind an ocean wave wrapping around rocks as it rushes onto shore—that's a bit like what I'm describing. This light is living, and it pulsated outward from the city center like laser beams that never diminish. But unlike a laser beam on earth, light in Heaven won't harm but only ministers to one and all from the essence of the one and only true God.

> *Then Jesus spoke to them again, saying, "I am the light of the world. He who follows Me shall not walk in darkness, but have the light of life"* (John 8:12).

I had only been in Heaven for a short time, but already I was baffled about how I could even survive the amount of light that was washing through me. It was beyond spectacular to experience. The light filled me with energy and love with each new wave.

Every sight and sound intensified in my being as I approached the opening in the massive wall. The gate was my access into Heaven's heart. It is where the light, the love, and the life originate. *I hope I'm allowed to go into the city*, was my growing desire.

As I drew closer to the wall, I was stunned at how much larger it was than I first thought. It was made up of a series of seven vertical walls—each layer pressed together, making up the magnificent whole. The outer layer of wall was about forty feet high, stair-stepping up to the center wall, which stood approximately two-hundred feet high. Surprisingly, at the base, the massive wall, when considered with all seven layers, appeared to be about as thick as it was tall.

The foundations of the wall of the city were adorned with all kinds of precious stones: the first foundation was jasper, the second sapphire, the third chalcedony, the fourth emerald, the fifth sardonyx, the sixth sardius, the seventh chrysolite, the eighth beryl, the ninth topaz, the tenth chrysoprase, the eleventh jacinth, and the twelfth amethyst (see Revelation 21:19-20).

As the light refracted through the lovely stones that made up this imposing barrier, the colors seemed to dance in the atmosphere, causing a kaleidoscope of various hues and creating a colorful effect that surrounded the city. The colors swayed and shimmered, generating a living rainbow that seemed to dance with the music. It was breathtaking.

With every movement I made, the colors made small adjustments. Each color contained multiple hues—with each one seeming to have its own personality. These many shades and hues moved and ministered to my heart—filling me with joy. They were alive—palpable and pulsating on melodies that filled the atmosphere.

As I continued closer to the colorful rows of stone, I could no longer see the top of the huge wall. Standing next to the base, I could see deep greenish hues in the bottom layer of stones, likely reflecting the lush grass that surrounded the wall.

The magnificent opening that had been my destination for some time became astoundingly more beautiful the closer I got. It was more than an opening. It was a royal gate—intricate, ornate, and gorgeous to behold. It had a gracefully arched opening forty to fifty feet high and about thirty to thirty-five feet wide. It stood open and unobstructed, granting entrance through the wall. There was no door. No barricade. Nothing to preclude my access into the city, at least so it appeared.

Streams of living light rushed outward through the opening as if in joyful escape. Light enveloped and ministered in a colorful display of love and energy to all who were touched by it.

CHAPTER 3

WONDERS OF HEAVEN

Also she had a great and high wall with twelve gates, and twelve angels at the gates, and names written on them, which are the names of the twelve tribes of the children of Israel.

—Revelation 21:12

The two angels who guided me appeared delighted at my joy in each discovery. They directed me to arrive at this location near the gate, at this exact time. There was an expectancy in their faces—as though something was preparing to announce itself. I moved toward the stunning entrance that graced the wall like a crown jewel.

THE GATE

The opening through the wall was opalescent in color and texture. It had the appearance of being coated in pearl, as if millions of these flawless gems had been liquefied and poured over the surface of the entire gateway and into the opening for as far as I could see. Wrapped around the entrance, embedded into the iridescent lining, was an intricate array of jewels interlaced with gold. It was a breathtaking framework of ornamentation, reminding me of an elaborate gold and jeweled crown.

> *The twelve gates were twelve pearls: each individual gate was of one pearl* (Revelation 21:21).

The light that shone through the mesmerizing pearl substance, like all the light I'd seen so far, was hypnotic. Every color imaginable gyrated in the atmosphere. The light shone and refracted through the jeweled stones to create a rainbow orb that filled the entire opening.

A single arched line of large gold letters was inlayed above the gateway, vibrating and shimmering with life. Embedded within the walkway that led into the gate were several additional lines of lettering made with transparent amber-colored gems. Though I could not read the words, I knew instinctively that they were important.

To the right of the entrance stood a majestic angel. He was towering—about nine feet tall—which made him larger than the angels who were accompanying me. This angelic guard exuded strength from his masculine frame. He was dressed similar to my escorts, in a long seamless white robe, but with a notable difference. Wrapped around his lower chest was a wide golden belt embossed with a large emblem in place of a buckle. His pale-colored hair, contrasting with his bronze complexion, was longer, falling almost to his shoulders. Another notable attribute of this imposing guardian of the gate was the light and love that radiated from him.

Our eyes met, and his welcoming expression seemed to indicate that I had been expected. I use the masculine gender only because the angels that I saw looked masculine, even though they were neither male nor female.

As I stepped toward the gate, the angel moved to the center of the opening, blocking my intended path. He stood firmly planted with his feet apart and with one arm outstretched, palm facing toward me, indicating that I was not allowed to proceed into the entrance.

I searched the angel's face for clues as to what was happening. But I saw only joy and acceptance. His eyes were full of kindness. His countenance radiated love. Then he pointed toward the right side of the opening where a columned pedestal stood.

> *Its gates shall not be shut at all by day (there shall be no night there).... But there shall by no means enter it anything that defiles, or causes an abomination or a lie, but only those who are written in the Lamb's Book of Life* (Revelation 21:25-27).

THE BOOK OF LIFE

Resting atop the golden stand was a massive book, the likes of which I had never seen. I don't know how I hadn't noticed it before. The book was astoundingly beautiful, bound in a cover made of solid pearl with gold lattice wrapped around the edges. Light poured out of it like vapor. As usual, my description is grossly inadequate, but what I'm trying to tell you is that light is not supposed to behave this way. Nevertheless, it did. The book was filled with living light that shone from within its cover and radiated from each page. For a moment, I wondered what this great volume could be and why the angel had directed me to it. But again, as quickly as the questions formed in my mind, my heart understood.

This was the Book of Life. Inside were the names of those allowed to enter Heaven. Unless my name was in this book, entry would not be permitted. Not now, not ever. Somehow I knew this as truth, and suddenly nothing was more crucial than finding my own name written within the pages of this book. Literally nothing was more important.

> *And if anyone's name was not found written in the book of life, he was thrown into the lake of fire* (Revelation 20:15 ESV).

I moved toward the golden stand, studying the cover of the book. I wondered about my own fate, *Is my name inside?* Then in a fluid movement the book opened itself to the one page where I could see my name written. There it was. My full name—first, middle, and last. Truthfully, I was a bit shocked. I knew that in recent years I'd become astoundingly selfish. I had begun putting my own desires ahead of God's. My mind questioned, *Do I really deserve to have my name in this book?*

In my youth, I had sincerely asked Jesus into my heart, and since that time had stayed in agreement with that decision. Waves of gratitude washed over me as I vividly remembered the night that I asked Jesus Christ into my life.

Several numbers were inscribed next to my name. Each character glistened and shimmered, scrolling across the page from right to left. Though many other names were present, and each page seemed filled, I couldn't read them. They looked faded and blurred, like they were grayed out. The only name that I found legible was my own: Dale Russell Black.

But I was confused by the numbers that were next to my name. Immediately, I thought there must be some mistake. I was born on January 1, 1950. This didn't correspond to the number I saw in the book. *Uh-oh. Maybe this isn't my name after all. Maybe it's a different Dale Black, and I'm not really in the book.*

And just like before, the answer was provided directly to my heart. In this case, the angel standing next to the book cleared my confusion. "No, Dale, not the day of your earthly birth. The first number is the day you were created by God—the day you were given life."

I paused and thought about what I had just learned. I contemplated the ramifications and the significance. In Heaven, the day of conception is what is important, not the day I was physically born.

"What about the other date?" I asked the angel.

"Do you not remember, Dale? Don't you recall the time when you invited Jesus into your heart? That is the day you were reborn. This is your spiritual birthday: June 29, 1961, the day you were born again."

I stared in awe at the numbers and my name. Oh, how glad I was that I had made that life-changing decision during the evening chapel service at summer camp when I was in the fifth grade.

Then a thought hit me. I gazed back at the book wondering why there was not a date for my death. *Clearly, I died—didn't I?*

Once again, the answer came. "You are eternal, Dale; you are not dead. You will never die." As I contemplated this response, I had to admit that, since I'd left my body, I sure didn't feel dead! In fact, I had never felt more alive.

There was great delight in the face of the gate's guardian. His smile turned to a grin as he stepped aside and motioned that I was permitted to enter the city of Heaven. Instinctively, I gave him a slight nod, then raised my arms, thanking God for this great and awesome privilege.

To my relief, my very own name was in this Book of Life. I had seen it and have forever been grateful and humbled.

> *The one who is victorious will, like them, be dressed in white. I will never blot out the name of that person from the book of life, but will acknowledge that name before my Father and his angels* (Revelation 3:5 NIV).

But I'm getting ahead of myself.

Before I share more of the wonders of Heaven with you, you'll want to know how I arrived at such a glorious place so you can understand why it had such a profound effect on me. You'll want to know what my life was like and why it was permanently changed. And by understanding these details, it's possible that your life might also be changed.

CHAPTER 4

CAPTAIN OF MY FATE

Whereas you do not know what will happen tomorrow. For what is your life? It is even a vapor that appears for a little time and then vanishes away.
—James 4:14

July 17, 1969—The Day before the Crash

Daybreak was fast approaching Southern California. My forest-green MGB convertible raced toward the Hollywood-Burbank Airport, screeching and hugging the curves of the familiar Pacific Coast Highway.

Despite a cloudless sky, the resident smog hung low over the city, creating a dreamlike scene in the early morning half-light. My sense of freedom was exhilarating. My fingers began tapping out the beat on the steering wheel as the radio blasted out my favorite song that year, "Born on the Bayou," by Creedence Clearwater Revival.

Catching my reflection in the rearview mirror, I smiled at the epaulet straps gracing the shoulders of my pilot's shirt. They reminded me that I was *cool*. I was following my destiny. I was on a quest toward becoming a professional aviator. Some pilots have epaulets with three stripes, some four, depending on their experience and position. The straps on my shirt were empty. Although I had earned my private pilot's license, stripes were for professional pilots, not for young pilots-in-training like me. But I wasn't worried about it. I knew my stripes would come. It was just a matter of time.

AN OBSESSION TO FLY

Ever since childhood, I had dreamed of becoming an airline pilot for a major US carrier. A trip around the world with my family in my early teen years had fueled my dream of adventure. By the time our TWA Boeing 707 had landed in Rome, I was hooked. The desire to fly a large jet, especially the four-engine 707, became a secret desire that grew into an outward obsession.

> *"For My thoughts are not your thoughts, nor are your ways My ways," says the Lord. "For as the heavens are higher than the earth, so are My ways higher than your ways, and My thoughts than your thoughts"* (Isaiah 55:8-9).

It's quite strange. Even as I tell you about this trip to the airport, it seems like it happened only yesterday. If I close my eyes, I still feel the wind whipping at my hair and the sensation of the soft leather knob of the gear shift in my grip. I can feel the solid movement of the MGB as it speeds down the road. I can smell the familiar LA smog on the freeway. Even at that early hour, I was wide awake, singing a snatch of each song that played over the airwaves of KRLA.

Some would say I was in my own world. But that would be an understatement. It was more than that. In my mind, I was captain of my fate, master of my universe. I had life completely figured out. I knew who I was and where I was going. To me, it only made sense that someday I would change the world. Go ahead. It's okay. Now is a good time to laugh.

Thinking back, it surprises me how impossibly naive I was, yet I thought I knew everything. I was young—nineteen. Most considered me a good student and excellent athlete—which was nice, but those were not the most important things in my life. Living my dream—*that* was at the top of my list.

I was a hardworking truck driver and mechanic in the family business, which paid me good money for my age. My dreams were costly—college tuition and aviation training, for starters. I was reasonably good-looking. At the time, I had two girlfriends, no debt, a sports car, and a future that, to me, looked as bright as the sun. I took flying lessons as often as I could afford. No time to waste. I was going places. Yep, living a dream all right. Or so I thought.

On the way to the airport that morning, an oncoming highway patrolman spotted my speeding MGB and turned in pursuit, siren blaring. I looked at the speedometer. *Oops.* But I knew just what to do. I'd done it a dozen times, and it usually worked. Performing a series of three quick right turns, I darted into an alley, parked, and turned the engine off. I ducked down out of sight until I heard the patrol car speed past. *Whew. Worked again.*

As the noise of the siren faded in the distance, I did what any nineteen-year-old would do. I laughed out loud. Now with a sizeable grin, I got back on the road with a renewed sense of invincibility. I wasn't a *bad* kid, just a bit of a rebel and a young man driven by big dreams. I never doubted that I could accomplish anything I set my mind to. And so far, so good. But very soon—and unexpectedly—my world would change in ways no one could have imagined, least of all me.

I continued on, staying under the speed limit until I glided through the gates of my destination. This airport—*any* airport—was sacred ground to me. It was like crossing an invisible threshold where I became a different person. This is where my dreams took flight—literally. Aviation was serious business. Here I felt more like an astronaut than a truck driver. It was the one area of my life where I submitted. In fact, it was the *only* place where I submitted. *Responsibility*—in the world of aviation—was my middle name.

I pulled up in front of the plush Pacific Airmotive Executive Aviation terminal. Yanking on the parking brake, I jumped out of the car without opening the door. I had arrived at a place where flying was the Holy Grail that opened the door to my biggest dreams.

Grabbing my pricey gray Samsonite briefcase full of aviation charts and tools of the trade, I headed toward the door. Pausing briefly, I picked a fresh flower from the garden.

"Hey! You can't do that!" Startled by the loud voice, I turned to see the scowling face of the gardener, pointing at me.

Without thinking much, I stood at attention and gave the gardener a full military salute. His confused face relaxed a little then turned to a slight smile as he waved me off in frustration. Cracking into laughter, I turned and hurried toward the terminal, flower in hand.

Once inside, I approached the reception desk holding the flower behind my back. *Will she be here? It is Thursday, right?* Just as my hope wavered, I spotted Linda working behind the counter—a gorgeous blond flight attendant in her twenties, dressed in a classy navy-blue and white uniform. Grinning, I presented the flower. "For you, beautiful."

She blushed.

Walking backward to keep Linda in my sights, I moved toward the door. *Perfect…she's smiling. Will she wave? Yes!*

SETTING UP IDOLS

Buoyed by my success, I turned and headed outside onto the tarmac. My focus shifted to the uniformed pilot wearing captain's epaulets who was just stepping down from a sleek twin-engine aircraft. It was Chuck Burns, my flight instructor, mentor, and friend. At age twenty-eight, with his muscular build and crew-cut hair, he looked like he could have been a professional football player, or maybe a model in a men's cologne commercial, dressed in his impeccable pilot's uniform, graced by his chiseled face and strong jaw.

I wanted to be just like Chuck—an athletic, good-looking, professional pilot with brains. This was a man I looked up to, a man I really liked. Chuck was a genuinely nice guy. And he had achieved so much already, with a bachelor's degree in engineering and a lot of logged flight time and experience. He had also earned something else I wanted ever so badly—the coveted Airline Transport Pilot (ATP) certificate. To me, the ATP certificate was like having a PhD in aeronautical science.

Besides all that, Chuck was married, had two kids, owned a lovely home, drove a beautiful car, and had lots of friends. I can't say it enough—I wanted to be just like Chuck. I wanted the life he was living. As if to prove his success, the next day he was heading up to San Francisco to interview for a pilot position with

United Airlines. *Wow. If I stay close and follow his advice, I'll get there, too. Hard work, lots of study, and patience, Dale.*

It was an honor to be inside Chuck's circle of influence. Of course, I was ecstatic to fly with him. He was teaching me, guiding me vocationally, and helping me build my flight hours.

That morning, Chuck gave me a slight smile as he noticed me heading in his direction. I practically jumped out of my shoes to jog over.

"Perfect day for flying, my friend," he said while inspecting the outside of the aircraft. "Did you get any sleep?"

I laughed as we climbed into the cockpit and took our seats. "There's no time for sleep. Drove my eighteen-wheeler *all night.* Barely made it here in time."

Once in the cockpit, Chuck shook his head, smiling while checking the instruments. "You work too much. Everyone else your age parties at night."

I shrugged. "Flying lessons and college tuition aren't cheap. Plus, I've got girls to impress."

Chuck looked at me with a grin. He understood. He had been the same way at my age—driven, self-made. Thinking back to the first time we met, I had sensed within minutes he and I were kindred spirits.

I was not ashamed of how hard I worked for my age. Getting paid for my labor gave me a sense of control over my future and the inner confidence that I could reach my goals. *Whatever I choose to do, I will do.*

> *Let no one deceive himself. If anyone among you seems to be wise in this age, let him become a fool that he may*

become wise. For the wisdom of this world is foolishness with God.... (1 Corinthians 3:18-19).

Being raised in a hardworking family business, I saw relationships built more around whatever the business needed than anything personal. Grandparents, parents, uncles, and cousins, we all pulled together to succeed. And we were close! If there was anything I understood growing up, it was hard work and teamwork. My dad also taught us the principles of positive thinking. He often gave us tapes to listen to on goal setting and success principles. Earl Nightingale's audio teachings served me well.

Like others, I was a product of my childhood. The seeds that had been planted in my life had produced fruit and lots of it, just not always the best kind.

Heaven has a way of implanting a plumb line, like a compass, in a person's heart. It certainly happened with me. It's like installing a new, revolutionary guidance system in an aircraft to keep it on its flight path. Heaven's perspective is now the predominant focus in every situation I encounter.

One doesn't have to visit Heaven to understand God's plan. His plan is written clearly in His Word. But prior to the crash, I hadn't been paying attention.

CHAPTER 5

CHASING DREAMS

*Delight yourself in the Lord, and He will give you the
desires of your heart.*

—Psalm 37:4

You may be wondering about my faith. Let me explain. My mother's family were strong Christians. My father and his entire family were devout Mormons. But in 1953, my dad invited Jesus Christ into his life, and from that moment forward, he was an amazingly different man.

Following Dad's experience, my parents and grandparents taught me the basics of the Christian life. And I invited Jesus Christ into my heart at summer camp when I was eleven. While growing up, I often participated in our church's teen youth group and several outreach ministries. The church my family attended was a huge part of my life, both socially and spiritually. But during my senior year of high school and on into college, I increased my focus on sports, education, adventure, social activities, and of course flying. And I had to work extra hard to earn the money I needed to control my destiny. So I no longer took time in my busy schedule to focus on God. Although I still attended church weekly, spiritually, I was undeveloped and immature.

> *We should no longer be children, tossed to and fro and carried about with every wind of doctrine,… but, speaking the truth in love, may grow up in all things into Him who is the head—Christ* (Ephesians 4:14-15).

What faith I did have didn't spill over into my life outside the church. Like my career goals—those were mine to control. And why would God care about those things anyway? Certainly, I respected God, but I didn't understand Him. I mean, who does? I didn't know the Bible well either. The countless sermons I heard all melded together in my mind as religious dos and don'ts. And I couldn't have told you anything accurate about Heaven or, for that matter, about hell either. Those were things for the old and infirm but had little to do with me and my life of success and adventure as a professional pilot someday.

On this particular Thursday, July 17th, Chuck and I were allowed to conduct a short orientation flight in the company's new twin-engine, ten-seat, Turbo Piper Navajo Chieftain. It was as beautiful as it was powerful, and I drooled over the opportunity to fly such sophisticated equipment.

At age nineteen, with barely over 100 hours of flight time in my logbook, I was not qualified or experienced enough to fly the Chieftain alone. But even at that point in life, I had already finished my first year of college, had a steady job as a truck driver on diesel bigrigs, and had earned a Private Pilot's Certificate. I had also completed the required training and was recommended to take the test for my Multi-Engine Aircraft Rating. I was well on my way to reaching my dreams.

The best part was that I had paid for it all myself, which gave me a feeling of pride and a sense of control. "The sky's the limit!" I would often say to friends and family.

For I say, through the grace given to me, to everyone who is among you, not to think of himself more highly than he ought to think, but to think soberly, as God has dealt to each one a measure of faith (Romans 12:3).

Months earlier, I had approached Chuck at the airport and convinced him to let me help. I would do all of Chuck's loading and unloading throughout the day. I'd clean and fuel the airplane, do the pre-flight, manage minor maintenance with the mechanics, and even drive the cargo van when needed. Basically, I'd do anything for Chuck—without pay—if, in return, he would allow me to ride along. I'd fly right seat—logging flight time as dual instruction, which was extremely valuable to a young aspiring pilot like myself.

This was a special day—a day I had longed for. It was the day Chuck allowed me to fly from the left seat. It was an honor to settle into the captain's chair. Chuck, sitting in the right seat, nodded, and I started the engines. The whine of the props revving up never ceased to bring chills of excitement.

"The freedom of flying never gets old, does it?" Chuck asked over the noise of the props.

"Nope. Never. My folks think I'm going to get this out of my system someday."

"When did the flying bug hit you?" Chuck asked.

I laughed, raising my voice to be heard over the roar, "Ever since I can remember, I wanted to be an airline pilot."

Under Chuck's direction, I taxied the Navajo toward the departure runway, and moments later our wings were lifting us into a cloudless sky.

I can recall the thrill I felt as the plane smoothly ascended higher and higher. Chuck and I would shout above the loud drone of the engines. Back in those days, we didn't use headsets like the pilots do now. It's no wonder pilots of that era are often hard of hearing in their later years.

While I was concentrating on the flying, Chuck asked me a haunting question. "So, your parents worry about you flying?"

I nodded. "Dad thinks flying is a *big* mistake. Mom worries about everything—what music I listen to, whether I need a haircut. Neither of them supports my dream."

"Is it worth it?"

"What do you mean?"

"Well, most airline pilots come from the military. Others have the GI bill, government loans, *or* parents who help financially—*something* for flying. You've got none of that. You work two jobs and take a full load in college. I'm just asking, is it worth it?"

Our eyes met, and I reeled in confusion. I had never considered the question. I was determined to be an airline pilot no matter what. *I wonder what Chuck is talking about?*

ASSAULTED DREAMS

Chuck and I flew for a while without talking. My mind flashed back to a conversation I'd had with my parents a couple weeks earlier. I had been nervously sitting in our picture-perfect living room across from my mom and dad. It was just the three of us. Mom was a lovely, vivacious blonde, young for being a mother of three older teens. And Dad, in his forties, was sort of a General Patton type—a tough leader. He was determined, arrogant, a driver, and a man who seldom smiled. For many, my father was downright intimidating.

Dad snapped, "You want to fly, Dale? Then what's your plan? You need to make a lot of money for this hobby of yours. Your mother and I certainly aren't paying for it."

"It's a *career*, not a hobby," I barked back. "And as usual, I'm not asking you for help. Not asking you guys for *anything*."

Dad shook his head in frustration. "I've spent my whole life building a business. A family legacy. Your brothers work there, so do your uncles and cousins. You want to just walk away from it all?"

I could see the irritation on his face, yet I fired back, "I don't want to grow old driving trucks. I'm going to be an airline pilot. I'm going to rule the sky."

"Oh, beautiful. That's just beautiful." Dad spat out the words sarcastically.

Abruptly I stood, moving toward the back door. "Can't I get a little support for my dreams? You guys just don't get it!" No one seemed to understand how important flying was to me.

Dad wouldn't let it go. "Dreams are dreams. They vanish by morning. Hard work's the key. Hard work got me where I am."

It was true. Dad had little formal education, yet had become a millionaire several times over. He was a hardworking man with an instinct for business. His Mormon upbringing, along with seeing his parents run their own business, had served him well. I respected him for what he had accomplished.

But I couldn't sit still and listen to my dreams being assaulted. They weren't going to vanish. I wouldn't let them. These dreams were real. My parents just didn't understand. I bolted from the room, slamming the door behind me. I guess Chuck was right by asking me if it was worth it. I *was* on my own. Even as important as flying was to me, maybe Chuck Chuck knew something I didn't—that I couldn't do it without help.

Pointing toward Lockheed Corporation's huge aviation and space complex, I blurted out, "The way I see it, man has conquered space, right? Putting a man on the moon in a few days. I mean it's time to dream big. Who knows…*we* could be up there one day."

"Where you gonna watch the moon landing?" Chuck asked.

"I'm scheduled to work, but I'll get out of it."

"Want to watch it at my house?"

I turned and grinned, "That'd be great."

Joy of Flying

Chuck allowed me to continue flying the airplane, and of course, I was thrilled. Under his direction from the right seat, he guided me over many of Southern California's well-known sights. We soared above Hollywood—marked by the brilliantly lit HOLLYWOOD sign. We flew over the famous round silhouette of the Capitol Records building, and Griffith Park Observatory. We turned, being careful to avoid the busy airspace over LAX, and continued flying at about 3,000 feet above the city of Pasadena. Below was the Rose Bowl, the football stadium where I had celebrated many birthdays. Being a New Year's Day baby had its perks.

I asked Chuck if we could fly over Pasadena College, where I could see my dorm building and the campus where much of my life unfolded in those days. Oh, the stories my dorm could tell if it could only talk.

Chuck asked me to turn southeast, heading over Orange County, where we looked down at Disneyland.

"Have you ever seen the fireworks display over Disneyland?" Chuck asked, as he continued looking through the windshield for traffic.

"Sure thing. Lots of times."

"No, I mean from the air. Have you ever flown over Disneyland at 9:00 p.m. and watched the fireworks from the air?" His gaze was focused below while using his hand motion to instruct me to bank the aircraft and circle the park. "You should do that sometime."

Then he motioned to turn back toward Burbank. As I adjusted our heading, we got a great view of LA's city center, where the largest buildings in downtown stood, including City Hall, the focal point of the television program *Dragnet*. All in all, it was a beautiful day for flying—a flight to remember.

When I think back to this flight, it really does *feel* like it happened yesterday. Memories come rushing back in…the sights, sounds, smells, and feelings…everything. I had so much focus at that point in my life. I saw the world as safe, exciting, and full of promise—one big adventure. This was one day before the crash—the last *normal* day of my life. It would take eight months after waking from a coma to even remember it.

This short and exciting flight would turn out to be my final flight of innocence.

And what happened next would take forty years to explain.

CHAPTER 6

I CAN'T BE DEAD

All flesh is as grass, and all the glory of man as the flower of the grass. The grass withers, and its flower falls away.

— 1 PETER 1:24

With a slight nod, Chuck motioned that he would take over the flight controls and bring us in for landing back at the Hollywood-Burbank Airport. As we descended, I noticed the familiar sight of a Lockheed C-130, a legend in aviation, parked on the tarmac. The Hercules was the huge four-engine turboprop military transport that carried soldiers and equipment to and from the raging war in Vietnam.

A full platoon of US Marines dressed in battle fatigues was marching in two lines up the open ramp of the aircraft's aft fuselage.

Chuck scoffed and muttered under his breath, "What a useless war."

That could be me soon. But if I have to go to 'Nam, I'll not go as infantry. I'll go as a bomber pilot.

In the back of my mind, my B plan was to go into the Air Force where I could fly. I preferred big and slow bombers to fast and nimble fighter jets. At an early age, I'd become a World War II aviation buff. Two uncles and many of my dad's friends had served in that war. Now, many of the guys with whom I had attended high school were already part of this new war in the jungles. A few of my friends had already been sent home in flag-draped coffins, including my good friend from our high school football team. *This war is real. And it's really ugly. But if I'm assigned, I'll do my duty for America as a pilot.*

Following the airplane crash, I would often go to Brookside Park in Pasadena, the baseball diamond where our college team practiced and played our home games. It was a familiar place where I could be alone and think. Baseball had always been a huge part of my life. My older brother, Don, was a baseball superstar. I had played somewhat in his shadow since we were kids in Little League. Still, I played a good shortstop and third base, and was a reasonably strong hitter. I was blessed with a rocket arm, so they said, and with a decent batting average, which included a few homers every season. I had received a college scholarship playing baseball. It was a sport that had added fun and balance to my intensely driven life.

The blunt trauma I experienced in the crash had caused me to lose much of my memory. I was working hard to recover the missing pieces and hoped that coming to the ballpark where I had spent so much time would help.

On one day, I loaded my wheelchair in the trunk of my MGB and drove myself to Brookside. After crawling into my wheelchair, I maneuvered slowly around the diamond and then past the bleachers. No one else was there—just me. It was perfect. Time to think and time to pray. Eventually, I ended up at the entrance to the dugout. With only an arm, one eye, and one leg barely working, I knew I couldn't get the wheelchair down the stairs. But I really wanted to sit inside the dugout where I had spent many hours at games and practices. Sliding out of the wheelchair on my backside, careful not to twist my injured back, I dragged myself down the stairs and up onto the familiar bench.

Ever since I had awakened from three days in a coma, I talked to God about everything. I shared every thought, every feeling. Whatever I was thinking turned into dialog between God and me. *Father, You said if I ask anything in Your name, You will give it to me, right? Dear God, please give me back my memory. Help me remember my life again.*

LOST MEMORIES

Instead of memories painting a colorful picture of life, my past was like a jigsaw puzzle. But my puzzle had gaping holes and missing pieces. My history was anything but clear. Strangely, I could remember early childhood and recall most of grade school, even much of middle school. But my memory of high school and college was a disaster—spotty at best.

Recent events were completely gone. One of the biggest assaults was the loss of what I had learned about aviation. I was horrified to realize that my flying career, which had only started the previous year, seemed to have vanished completely. Though I still had the license saying I was a pilot, I couldn't remember the most basic aspects of flying. And the crash itself? That had dissolved into oblivion along with everything surrounding it.

At the same time, something else happened—something strange but wonderful. Since the crash, I'd become a totally different person. Inside my heart, everything had changed. I didn't understand it with my head, but I knew I had made a 180-degree shift—from the inside out.

> *Therefore, if anyone is in Christ, he is a new creation; old things have passed away; behold, all things have become new* (2 Corinthians 5:17).

I was acutely aware the changes in me had to do with God and Heaven, but at that time, I didn't understand why; at least my brain couldn't remember. It felt like the memories were near, hovering just out of reach. I so badly wanted to harness these events that had caused such a transformation on the inside. I knew the crash had affected everything. *But why? How?*

Right after the crash—I mean, seconds after impact—my *spirit* observed the aftermath of the crash scene, including three seemingly dead bodies. At times, I was hovering just a few feet over the ground, and at other times, it was more like ten or fifteen feet above. Oddly enough, I was not emotional about what I was witnessing—not in the least. I also wasn't worried. But I was curious and somewhat confused. The world I had known had changed in ways I didn't understand.

I can't be dead…because I've never felt more alive. And then it hit me: *I'm not my body. I'm a spirit. I have a soul. And I used to live in a body.* Before the crash, I had it all mixed up. My understanding had been backward. But at the exact moment I saw my own dead body, I began thinking new and revolutionary thoughts.

Once I experienced this "out of body" event, once I learned this *truth*, my entire world changed. I'm convinced this is what happens to everyone when they die. Suddenly, the dead realize that they are spirits; they have souls, and they *used* to live in a body.

> *Now may the God of peace Himself sanctify you completely; and may your whole spirit, soul, and body be preserved blameless at the coming of our Lord Jesus Christ* (1 Thessalonians 5:23).

At every doctor's appointment, I would ask the doctor about my lost memory. He repeatedly informed me of the seriousness of the head trauma I had sustained, reminding me how those same injuries had killed the other two pilots. Memory loss, I was told, was to be expected, and I should be grateful for the things that I *could* remember. Furthermore, my brain was working well enough that I could still function.

I was grateful in my heart but frustrated in my mind. Much of the person I used to be—the old Dale Black—had vanished just like my old memories.

While sitting in the home field dugout that day, suddenly a new piece of the puzzle flashed vividly into my mind. It was like a hole burst open to let a memory rush back in. Recounting it with great focus, I savored the details. It was a baseball game—I was in my uniform, number 21, and playing shortstop. I had just fired a "smoke ball" to first base, stopping a runner. The crowd was applauding. I looked up to see my parents in the stands. Mom was jubilant—standing and clapping. Dad remained seated, unsmiling. As a driven businessman, his mind and body were seldom in the same place. But at least he was there. I was appreciative of his support on that level.

My newfound memory continued. The scoreboard showed the game was now in the bottom of the ninth. Batting third in the lineup, I stepped up to the plate and hit a curveball for a double on the first pitch, driving in the winning run. *Wow, Lord, thank You. What a great memory!*

At least now, with lots of prayer and some prompting, I was finally getting a few memories back.

As I analyzed my past, I realized how I had taken almost everything for granted. Prior to the crash, I had been gliding through life in many ways. I must admit that many things came easy for me. I was naturally athletic and had always excelled in sports. Up to this point, I had worked hard and gotten good grades and didn't see why I couldn't be and do whatever I wanted.

After the crash, my memory was such a mess I wondered if I would ever remember even the simple things—like my license plate or pilot's license number. Things that were easy to memorize before the crash were seemingly impossible to recall or memorize now.

I thought about the most important things—my spiritual life heading the list. In that department, I'd call myself bankrupt. I had always intended to clean up my act with God—someday—after I achieved the things that were important to me. But there was a lot of living to do first. And I needed to get ahead of the pack. Looking back, I had been a sorry excuse for a Christian, foolishly sitting on the throne of my own life, sidestepping God's will for me.

After the crash and my visit to Heaven, I was almost the opposite. My perspective on everything about life had changed. Yet with my brain injury, I still didn't understand *why*. All I knew was that now I was looking at the world and my life through my *heart*.

PHOTOS

Dale, age eleven—7Up Stars Little League Baseball

Don and Joyce Black (Dale's parents)

Senior picture, Western High School, Anaheim, CA 1968

Some of the trucks Dale drove and managed in the family business

Grandpa and Grandma (Russell & Neva) Price about 1980

Dale in his 1964 MGB prior to the crash

College Baseball Team—Dale #21

Playing college baseball in 1968 prior to the crash

A Piper Navajo similar to the one that crashed

TWA Boeing 707-331B N28727

The Boeing 707 is a mid-sized, long range, narrow-body, four-engine jet airliner, with a passenger capacity up to 219 and a range of 5,750 miles. Dale fell in love with the idea of becoming a pilot at age fourteen when his family flew on a Boeing 707.

Portal of the Folded Wings Shrine to Aviation.
Helicopter news photo of the crash.

Valhalla Memorial Cemetery - Portal
of the Folded Wings Shrine (crash site).

Cockpit instrument panel of crashed aircraft,
where Dale's body landed.

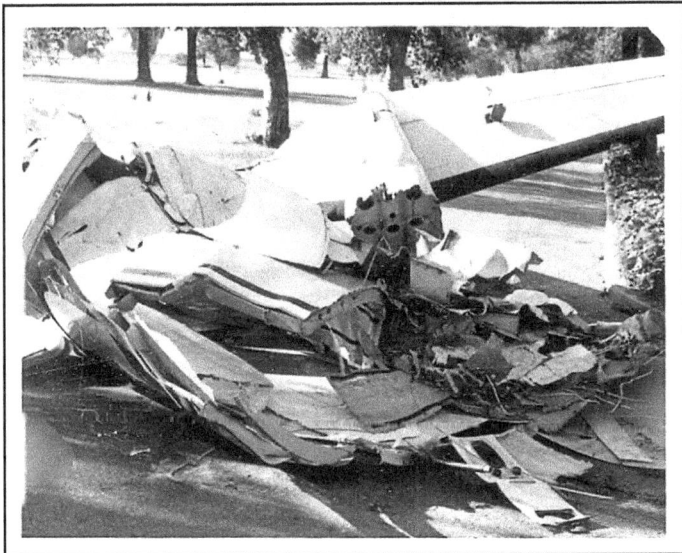

Tail section of the crashed Navajo aircraft

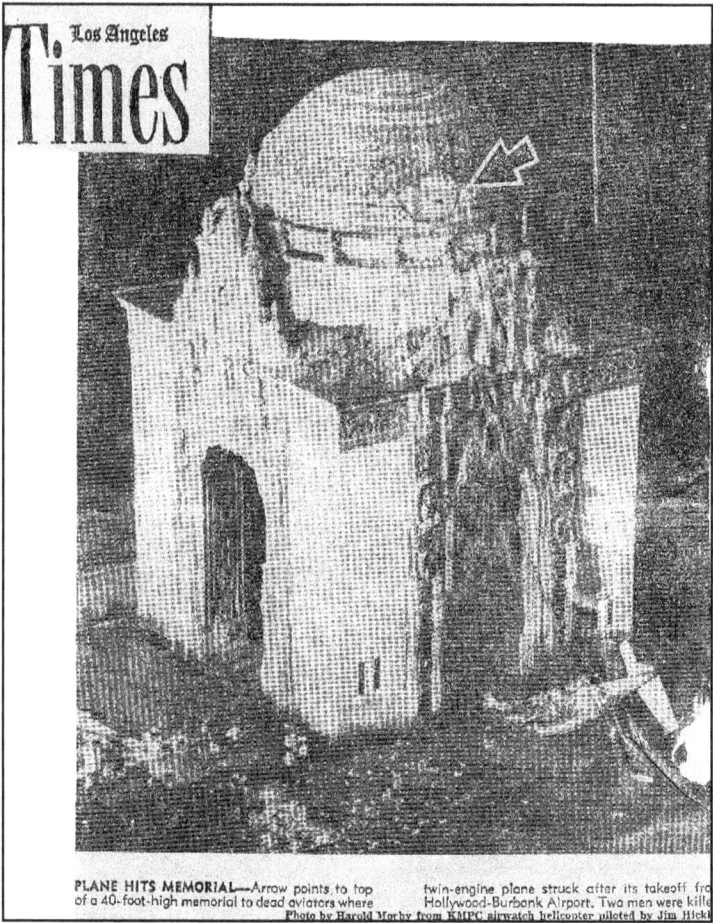

PLANE HITS MEMORIAL—Arrow points to top of a 40-foot-high memorial to dead aviators where twin-engine plane struck after its takeoff fro Hollywood-Burbank Airport. Two men were kille Photo by Harold Morby from KMPC airwatch helicopter piloted by Jim Hick

Portal of the Folded Wings Shrine, photo of crash in the *LA Times*

Fate? Coincidence? Or cruel irony? The wreckage of a Piper Navaho re- mains under inscription "Portal of the Folded Wings." Photos by Gene Howard

Portal of the Folded Wings Shrine crash site in the *LA Times.* Caption reads, "Fate? Coincidence? Or cruel irony? The wreckage of a Piper Navaho remains under Inscription 'Portal of the Folded Wings.'"

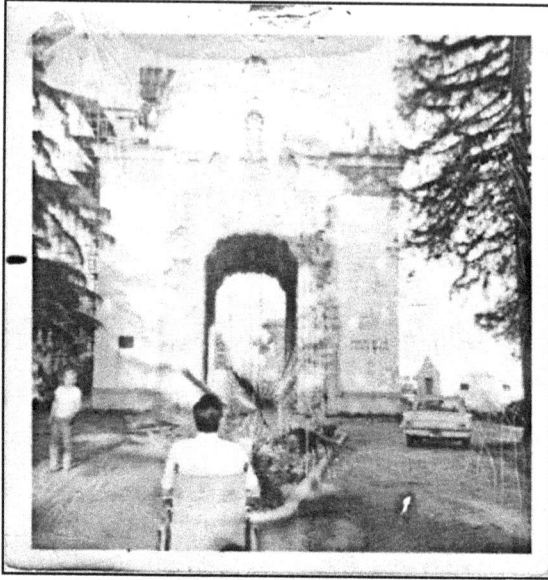

First visit to the site of the crash

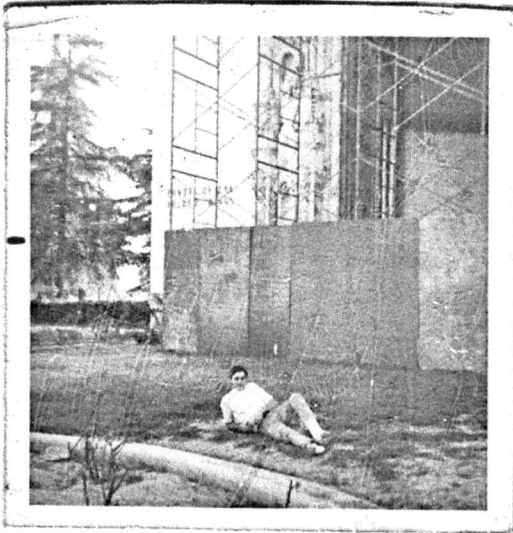

Portal still being repaired eleven months after crash

Dale with Chuck's Piper Aztec several months after the crash

First class FAA medical passed on July
18, 1970. Exactly one year after crash.

July 18, 1976—Dale flies as pilot-in-command
in another Navajo for the first time since the crash

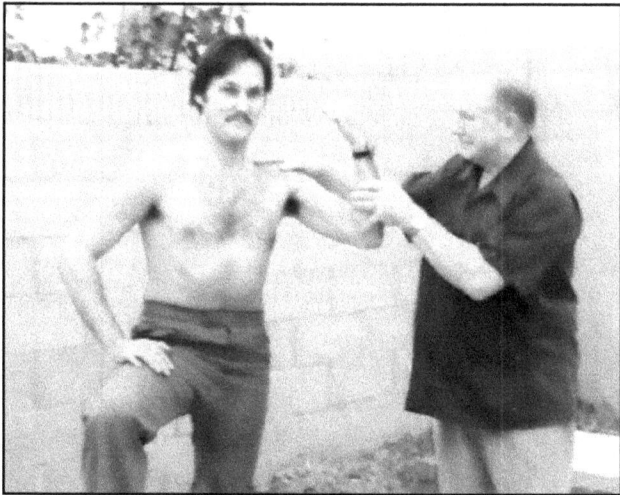

Dr. Graham admiring the miracle
of Dale's shoulder—1978

Dale and Capt. Bob fly SD3-30 on Dale's
retirement flight from Golden West Airlines.
Passengers: Don and Joyce (Dale's parents),
Paula, Eric, and Kara Black—1979

First day, first flight as TWA Boeing 707 Flight Engineer
on tenth anniversary of crash—July 18, 1979

Dale and Paula in TWA Boeing-747 at LAX

Dale and Dr. Graham in TWA Boeing-747
July 18, 1981

Dale becomes FAA Citation Jet ATP Examiner 1982

Dale, Kara, Eric, and Paula—1992

Giving testimony to airline personnel in Dale
and Paula's airplane hangar—Long Beach, CA

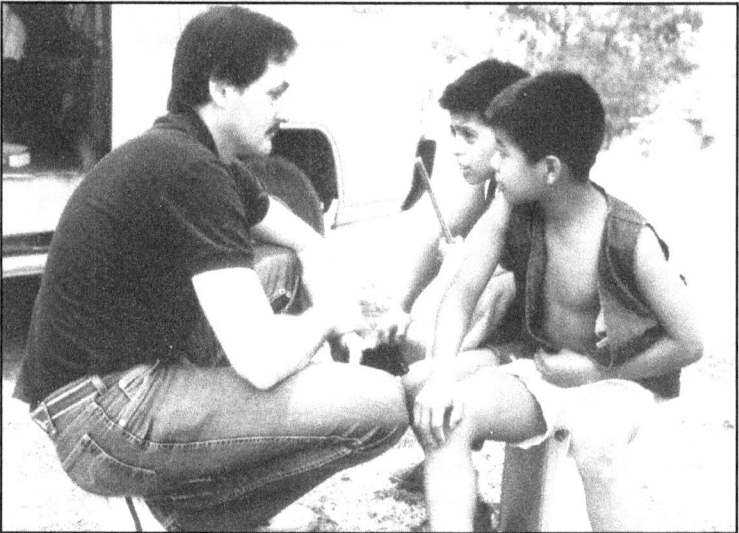

Dale shares Jesus with thousands in South America—1975

Dale and Paula with ministry team—Israel 1982

Flying a ministry group in 1980s

Dale and Paula at orphanage they built in Guatemala 1984

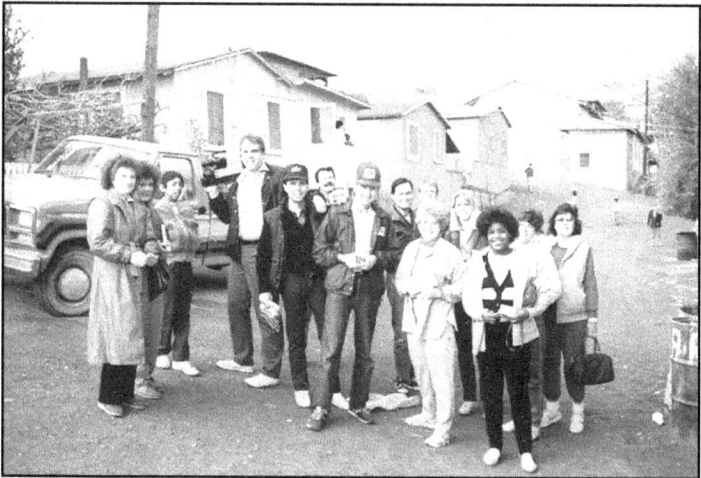

Dale and Paula lead a missionary and medical
team to a remote island off Mexican coast

Dale and Paula lead Mexico ministry—1989

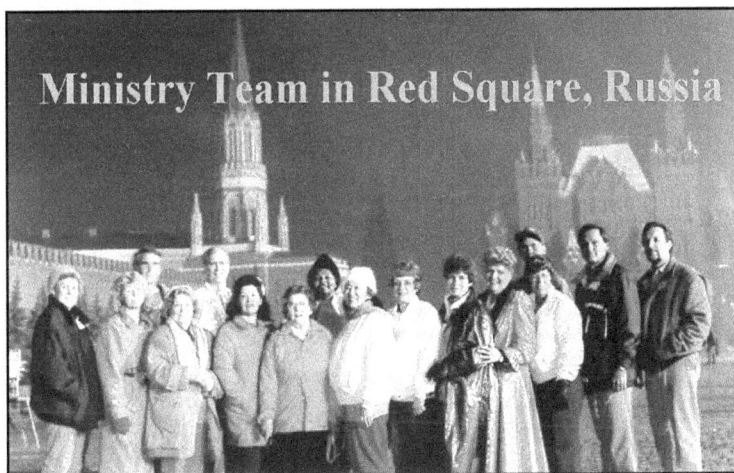

The second ministry team Dale led to Russia in 1990

Dale and Paula in Boeing 737—July 18, 1995

Paula, Dale, Kara, Deborah, and Eric—1997

CHAPTER 7

LAST DAY OF "NORMAL"

*For I know the thoughts that I think toward you, says
the Lord, thoughts of peace and not of evil, to give you a
future and a hope.*
—Jeremiah 29:11

Often, I am asked, "Why? Why did God allow you to experience such a horrible accident? If and God wants good things for us, why did you endure such terrible injuries in a crash?"

As an airline pilot, I learned that if I was flying from Los Angeles to Hawaii, I could not just set the heading once and then relax until it was time to land. There were hundreds of times throughout the flight that our plane would drift off track due to winds or other factors. Maybe only one degree, but if that one degree was not corrected, it would cause us to completely miss Hawaii and run out of fuel somewhere over the Pacific Ocean. Continual corrections are critical to staying on course and safely reaching any destination.

Well, my life was going off course in the most important area—my spiritual life. I had respect for God. I wanted to please

Him. But I had gradually put myself on the throne of my life, and He was relegated to the backseat by my own choosing.

God loved me too much to allow me to continue off course. If I had continued on the heading I was on, with the small choices I was continually making, I would have been in serious danger. Now, I am not saying that God caused the crash. No, the accident was pilot error on multiple levels. But God allowed me to go through a horrible accident and used it to bring me back home. God used the crash to put me back on the right path so I wouldn't miss my ultimate destination—Heaven. He miraculously preserved my life through what the NTSB considered a non-survivable accident. Then, as I pursued Him, He ministered truth to me and healing to my body, restoring me and even restoring my dream of becoming an airline pilot.

But seek first the kingdom of God and His righteousness, and all these things shall be added to you (Matthew 6:33).

But let's go back to before the crash, before everything shifted. One of my fondest memories was music. I grew up in a musical family. My mom had a beautiful voice and sang as she went about her day. Music was always playing on the radio or record player—like Frank Sinatra or Doris Day, Dean Martin or Perry Como—which I enjoyed. But that was Mom's music. I really loved Elvis, the Beatles, and Creedence Clearwater Revival. I played them nonstop on the eight-track in my car. And whenever I drove with the top down—which was often—the volume was all the way up.

That's how it was early on the morning of July 18th—the day everything changed. I remember the song. It was a new one by

Elvis Presley called "Suspicious Minds." The lyrics were probably written about the suspicions of two lovers. But to me it had
deeper meaning. The words were a sign of the times.

In 1969, America was living through extreme times—having
some of its *best* days and, at the same time, its worst. We were
reaching into space and headed to the moon, which had a unifying and rallying effect on the country. That same year the
Boeing 747 was introduced. So was the supersonic Concorde
SST. Although less known at the time, that year the internet got
its first successful connection in Menlo Park, California.

There were signs of social implosion in America during
this time. We were wrapping up a turbulent decade of protests
and riots. There was also a uniting force among many in the
fight against global communism. Then there was the American involvement in Vietnam. While there were those who were
vociferous in their condemnation of US policy in South Vietnam, a 1968 Gallup poll showed that 46 percent of Americans
approved of President Johnson's handling of the war, with 50
percent believing that it was essential to combat the expansion
of communism in Southeast Asia.

By the end of the '60s, however, seeds of distrust were growing, and many were becoming suspicious of the government. The
anti-war movement was almost in full swing—especially among
young people who had lost confidence in the honesty of the
country's leaders. At the same time, racial divisions grew as some
tried to bring change.

But in the middle of all the shifting culture and dramatic
events, I was boldly confident in myself and my personal life's
path. I had limitless hope for *my* future success.

LIFE OFF COURSE

The evening before the crash, at the family home in Rossmoor, California, I was sitting at the dinner table with Dad, Mom, and my brothers, Don and Darrell. The sound of Walter Cronkite's voice describing the imminent launch of Apollo 11 drifted in from the television in the adjoining living room. Cronkite was a trusted grandfather-like figure to me and countless others.

I had a personal fascination with the Saturn V rocket—the 36-story, five-engined rocket that would take the Apollo 11 spacecraft, along with Neil Armstrong, Buzz Aldrin, and Mike Collins, to the moon. Producing 7.5 million pounds of thrust at liftoff, it was (and still is) the largest and most powerful rocket ever launched.

Mom's voice interrupted my thoughts, bringing my focus back to the family conversation. "How did your first year of college wind up?"

Darn. Why did she have to ask me that?

"Not so great…"

Dad's voice interrupted with a boom. "He's out, Joyce. Out for good." Dad's disdain dripped from every syllable.

How did this conversation end up about me? I frantically glanced at my brothers, looking for any thread of support.

Mom gasped. "What does that mean?" Her head spun in my direction. "That's not true, is it?"

I shrugged my shoulders without looking up. "Well, sort of."

"It's permanent. He threw it all away." Dad's words stung. "He's off the baseball team. Lost his scholarship. Got expelled from college. He's finished."

"Back off, Dad. I was just having a little fun." I tried to minimize my litany of failures. What was it? Why did I have such a lack of respect for authority?

"Some practical joke." Dad leaned toward Mom, "He kidnapped the freshman class president. Flew him to the Mojave Desert and left him there tied up—helpless. Who does that kind of stuff?"

Mom gasped. "What?" Her eyes widened as she stared in disbelief.

My brother Don couldn't resist adding to my humiliation. "I heard Dale left him with a snakebite kit, half a sandwich, and a dime for a phone call. I mean, what more would the guy need?"

Don and Darrell roared with laughter until Dad's glare silenced them both. Mom's mouth hung half open.

Don continued to comment on my situation as I shifted miserably in my chair. "Dale's been on the hot seat ever since he blew up the dean's front lawn with a stick of dynamite."

Why did Don have to tell everyone that? What about the unwritten rule? What happens on campus stays on campus. This is home—it's supposed to be off limits.

My brothers continued to snicker while Mom sat silent with horror on her face.

Dad shook his head in disgust. "Now maybe Uncle Sam will send you over to 'Nam."

Poking at my food without looking up, I spoke softly, "It was just a harmless prank."

Mom reacted. "Vietnam? You need your student deferment, don't you?"

"The military will do him some good," Dad prodded, hoping for a reaction from me.

"Look, you guys, I'll get into another college—this time on a football scholarship. Plus, I'm getting my commercial pilot's license anyway, so don't worry about me."

"Oh, there's another great idea," Dad retorted. "Then you can get shot down over the jungles of Vietnam."

"Don't say that," Mom snapped back. Then she tried to shift the conversation. "I thought we were going to watch the astronauts on TV? I baked a pie."

Abruptly shoving my chair back, I stood up. "I gotta get some air." Bolting out the sliding door into the backyard, I slammed the glass door so hard it's a wonder it didn't shatter into a thousand pieces. I wouldn't have minded if it had. It would have felt great in that moment to hear an explosion of glass.

Standing alone in the backyard, I looked up into the night sky. The flashing lights of jet airliners going to and from LAX were crossing overhead a little to the north of our Los Alamitos home. *That's where I'll be someday. Up there flying one of those giant jets. I don't fit down here, that's for sure. I belong up there…up in the sky!*

I looked back through the sliding glass door to see Mom and Dad having an intense conversation. Although I couldn't hear the words, I knew they were talking about me. That evening, it felt like I belonged to a different family. *Maybe I'm adopted and no one told me. That would explain so much. I just don't fit. I wish I could just fly away.*

Eventually, I opened the sliding door to reenter my world and face the music. The kitchen was empty. I stood alone listening to the voice of Walter Cronkite from the television in the other room: "Man is about to launch himself for a trip to the moon. Sitting there atop the great Saturn rocket are the three astronauts. My palms are sweaty...." Cronkite continued reporting as he shared his personal perspective on the momentous event.

Slowly, I moved into the living room where the family was gathered around the television. I sat down on the carpet, up close to the TV. These next moments were going to be important—the launch of the Apollo 11 mission. I felt as if it were me sitting in the tiny capsule atop the massive glistening white rocket. The entire country was holding its breath. I was barely breathing, my eyes fixed on the black-and-white images on the screen, anxiously waiting to see what would happen next.

CHAPTER 8

WELCOME TO ETERNITY

But God said to him, "Fool! This night your soul will be
required of you; then whose will those things be which
you have provided?"
—Luke 12:20

JULY 18, 1969—THE DAY THAT CHANGED EVERYTHING

My MGB once again sped toward the familiar Hollywood-Burbank Airport for my early morning flight. As I glided through the airport gate, I was back in the center of my dreams. The huge familiar letters on the terminal glistened in the morning sunlight: "Pacific Airmotive Corp." Dozens of private luxury jets, owned by movie stars and corporate bigwigs, were neatly positioned across the tarmac.

I had often eyed these gorgeous pieces of flying machinery, touching them, dreaming about what it would be like to pilot one with that much power and class. Occasionally I met one of the elite pilots of these jets and sometimes got a personal tour inside and out.

Bob Hope's Learjet was there. Sometimes I'd see Frank Sinatra's, too. One of the most luxurious airplanes that was based there belonged to my mom's favorite movie star, Cary Grant. The handsome, athletic, often humorous, and much-beloved star had his private DC-3 parked near the entrance to our terminal. I'll never forget almost drooling the day I was escorted inside of it for a tour. The interior was lined in plush Italian leather trimmed with ivory and silver and gold décor throughout. Even the levers on the toilet were plated in gold. *What a way to travel. Someday I'll own one of these. Mine might even be a jet.*

> *Do not lay up for yourselves treasures on earth, where moth and rust destroy and where thieves break in and steal; but lay up for yourselves treasures in heaven, where neither moth nor rust destroys and where thieves do not break in and steal. For where your treasure is, there your heart will be also* (Matthew 6:19-21).

I laugh today remembering my youthful perspective on life. But how could I have known then that earthly beauty pales to that which awaits us in Heaven? As the apostle Paul wrote,

> *Eye has not seen, nor ear heard, nor have entered into the heart of man the things which God has prepared for those who love Him* (1 Corinthians 2:9).

Doomed Flight

That early Friday morning, as I walked briskly toward the twin-engine Navajo we were scheduled to fly, I noticed some guy a couple years older than me, loading bags of bank checks into our aircraft. The markings on the side of his van read "United Clearings."

"Can I help?" I asked him.

"Sure thing. Thanks." He picked up another duffel from the van and tossed it my direction. It landed at my feet with a heavy thud. Our daily cargo was made up of thousands of bank checks we transported to various locations up and down the state.

Picking up a couple of the large bags, I tossed them into the back of the plane. Noticing some loose stacks of checks from a broken box in the van, I quickly bundled them up and tucked them into one of the canvas bags, throwing it into the plane along with dozens more.

Once the cargo was loaded and secured, I climbed into the cockpit and sat in the right seat. With checklist in hand and radio power on, I began twisting the knobs to set up the radios and navigation instruments. Then I checked the entire cockpit in preparation for our flight, just as Chuck had trained me. This was all part of the "Before Takeoff Instrument Setup" and would save Chuck time while giving me valuable experience.

Out of the corner of my eye, I spotted Chuck through the windshield. This morning something was going to be different. Standing next to Chuck was a man in his forties, looking slightly unshaven and rugged, dressed in civilian clothes. *Who's that guy? I better get outside and see how Chuck wants to handle things.*

"Dale, I want you to meet Gene. He's related to the boss." They both chuckled. "He's also a pilot with the Fresno Police and will be flying with us today instead of the Chief Pilot."

"Oh…okay. Nice to meet you, Gene."

I extended my hand, but Gene gave me a strange look and rejected the handshake. *What's his problem?* Maybe my hand was dirty from having checked the engine oil and fuel earlier. I wasn't sure, but I reached down and wiped the grease on my sock. *There. That fixes that.*

Chuck placed a hand on top of the engine cowl. "Dale, have you done the pre-flight and engine run-ups yet?"

"Yes, sir. And no, sir. The pre-flight is done. Cargo loaded and secure. But I did *not* complete the engine run-ups."

I didn't need to call him *sir*. It was a bit over the top, and I knew it. But it *was* appropriate, and Chuck seemed to appreciate it. In those days, the professional aviation world operated a lot like the military. Most of the airline pilots who were flying at the time were World War II vets. Still, Chuck was the only person I referred to with a *sir*. Such was my respect for him.

Gene looked in my direction. "You going to be my copilot today?"

I looked over at Chuck. Wait a minute, this wasn't the plan. I thought Chuck would be flying.

"He'll fly right seat," Chuck responded. Chuck directed his comment to Gene but spoke loudly enough for me to hear. "We'll go north to Santa Maria, Coalinga, then Fresno."

"Sounds like a plan," Gene replied.

The three of us climbed aboard the sleek Piper Navajo.

What I'm going to tell you next was lost from my memory for many months after the crash. Some people, no doubt, after a traumatic accident, don't want to remember. In contrast, I wanted very badly for all my memories to return. Eventually, almost everything did return—sometimes in horrifying detail.

Once my brain adequately healed, memories came flooding back—giving explanation to what was already *burned* into my heart. And once these memories returned, my mind and my heart were finally in sync.

With that said, here's what happened next. I can picture exactly who was where and what each of us was doing as if it were yesterday.

Gene was fastening his seat belt and getting settled in. He was in the left seat, normally the flying pilot's chair. I was buckled into the right seat, the copilot's chair. Chuck, who was responsible for the flight, was sitting slightly behind both of us on a temporary third seat, monitoring our every move. These details would become important for investigators later.

Gene called out, "Starting the right." He pressed the overhead switch, engaging the starter. The right engine spat and coughed, kicking to life, then settling into a nice hum.

"Starting the left," Gene repeated the procedure until the left engine matched the right. With both engines whirring at idle, it sounded like a musical symphony. Oh, how I loved the harmonic sound of two engines at idle thrust. To me, the only thing better was the roar heard at takeoff power.

My heart raced as I spotted a PSA Boeing 727 touching down in front of us. PSA was based in San Diego and known as "The World's Friendliest Airline," with a reputation among pilots as a fun place to work. Every airplane even had a large smile painted on its nose.

The roar and vibration of the 727 jetliner screaming into reverse thrust as it braked, filled our cockpit. I leaned toward Gene and announced my goal, "Someday I'll fly one of those."

"Everybody's got a dream," Gene replied.

The weather was perfect for our early morning flight. The wind was calm and the sky was crystal clear. Adrenaline pumped through my veins as we taxied toward the runway.

Chuck leaned into the cockpit, "Dale, tell ground control we'd like an intersection departure."

Gene spoke up abruptly, "Thanks, but I'll handle the radios." He reached across the cockpit, flipping the radio frequencies OFF then ON.

Chuck seemed unsettled by Gene's behavior and leaned forward. "Everything okay, Gene?"

"Everything's fine. Just checking."

Chuck responded in a firm voice, "Tell ground we're going to stop our taxi!"

I grabbed the mic preparing to speak to ground control just as Chuck tapped me on the shoulder. "Dale, let's trade places."

"Trade places? Right here?"

"Right here."

Chuck had decided he needed to be in the cockpit for the flight. After all, he was the official pilot-in-command. I'm sure he was trying to satisfy his boss by letting Gene fly that morning. I also think Chuck was thinking about me when he let me sit in the right seat. He knew how hard I worked without pay, how much I loved flying, and what it meant for me to log flight time and gain the flight experience. But something had changed his mind—something important enough to make him decide to exchange seats while we were taxiing.

Since the crash, I have flown for 48 years, logging over 18,000 hours of flying experience in a myriad of different aircraft. Most of my time was spent as an airline pilot instructor and accident-prevention aviation safety counselor. From a professional perspective today, it is clear to me that Chuck was in error. As pilot-in-command, he should have been in the cockpit the entire time. I am also convinced that, if Gene had not been on board that day, the crash would have never happened. There were a lot of things wrong on that flight, even before we took off.

The chief pilot was also in error. You don't send a pilot to fly your flight because he's your relative or because you want to be lazy for a day. I was also in error—just too inexperienced to realize it at the time. I should have never allowed myself to get in an airplane with no official seat for a third pilot. Our temporary seat, which Chuck had made out of cargo, was not approved. We all made mistakes in judgment but thought we could get away with them.

Our aircraft stopped on the taxiway with both props still spinning—engines at idle. For a moment, I considered getting out of the airplane, but I knew that would be a huge inconvenience for Chuck, who was trying to stay on schedule. I remember squeezing past Chuck as he moved into the cockpit to sit in the right seat and I moved back behind. I settled on top of the temporary third seat with my knees extended slightly into the cockpit and my feet flat on the floor.

As Chuck fastened his seat belt, he leaned toward Gene, "When's the last time you flew?"

"I'm current," Gene shot back.

Chuck glanced at me, our eyes locking for a second.

"That doesn't exactly answer my question."

Gene snapped, "Don't worry. I got it."

The tension in the airplane was palpable. Chuck paused, then spoke to Gene in a commanding voice, which he normally held in reserve, "Gene, you're still flying. But I'll handle the radios."

Chuck pressed the mic button and radioed the Burbank tower. As always, I was glued to his every word. I would always study not only *what* Chuck said but *how* he said it.

"Burbank tower, Navajo Five-Zero-Yankee ready for takeoff, runway one-five. Intersection departure."

The tower radioed back, "Navajo Five-Zero-Yankee, Burbank tower, after departure turn right heading two-four-zero. Climb and maintain three thousand. Departure Control on one-two-four point six-five. Intersection departure approved. Wind two-one-zero at five knots. You're cleared for takeoff, runway one-five."

Gene spoke up for all to hear, "Roger, we're rolling." Gene maneuvered the airplane onto the runway.

Chuck responded back, "Roger. We're cleared to go, runway one-five, right heading two-four-zero, maintain three thousand, departure on twenty-four sixty-five. Navajo Five-Zero-Yankee."

Gene pushed the throttles forward, and the aircraft sprang down the runway. Our twin-engine aircraft accelerated, bouncing a bit as we picked up speed. Finally, we lifted into the air, rising skyward into the morning light toward the Hollywood Hills.

To give perspective, we were flying south of what is now called the Bob Hope (Hollywood-Burbank) Airport. If we had continued flying on runway heading, our flight path would have taken us almost directly over the back side of the Hollywood sign, nestled on the top of the nearby Hollywood Hills.

Gene commanded, "Positive rate. Gear up."

Chuck reached forward and lifted a lever with a small wheel on it. "Gear coming up."

It *feels* strange even today as I recount the takeoff, and I'm not exaggerating when I say that, within about five seconds, I sensed something was wrong. For years, I couldn't remember just exactly what it was, but an unmistakable uneasiness hit almost immediately. Within a few more seconds, major problems became obvious.

AIRPLANE CRASH

We were about 100 feet above the ground when an unfamiliar whine flooded my ears. The engines sounded disturbingly out of sync. We were airborne, but something was horribly wrong. Although both engines were screaming at full power, we were no longer climbing. The plane struggled for altitude like a featherless bird flapping helplessly at the sky.

Scanning the instrument panel, I frantically searched for clues.

"You're too slow. *Lower the nose!*" Chuck barked out the words.

Both engines strained at maximum power, desperately attempting to keep the plane from falling back to earth.

Chuck yelled, "Pitch it down! Lower the damn nose!"

Huge trees instantly filled the windscreen. Both engines screeched with a sickening, out-of-sync, high-pitched shrill.

"I've got it!" Chuck yelled as he lunged for the flight controls. *"My airplane. I've got the controls!"*

Gene wouldn't let go. I watched as Chuck and Gene wrestled for control of the airplane.

Then I heard the unthinkable. "Let's land in that clear area over there!" Chuck spat out the words as he pointed toward an expanse of green grass stretching out before us.

I felt momentary relief. We're going to crash, but we'll be okay.

My eyes riveted to watch in horror as Chuck's white-knuck-led fists wrestled with the flight controls, trying desperately to overpower Gene. Chuck yanked the yoke full aft and all the way to the left in one lightning motion.

Then I heard Chuck whisper in a surrendered tone, "Oh, my God." Those would be his final words on earth.

CHAPTER 9

DEATH: A SPIRITUAL DIMENSION

For now we see in a mirror, dimly, but then face to face. Now I know in part, but then I shall know just as I also am known.
—1 Corinthians 13:12

Everything moved in slow motion. We were flying too low. I could see 100 foot treetops above us as our wings snapped branches like kindling. There was a loud *pop* as our plane spun in a new direction. My eye caught a fleeting glimpse of Gene's face, frozen in horror.

The grassy open space that had offered us hope moments before was instantly replaced with a huge building directly in our path. As I gripped the back of the pilot's seats in front of me, the tree branches gave way to the blue and gold colors of a mosaic tiled dome. I caught a fleeting glimpse of sculpted human-like figures—with their arms extended, as if welcoming us in death. It was my last image before our explosive collision.

In hundreds of nightmares following the crash, I heard the explosion of noise, tearing metal, engines screaming. I would wake up drenched in sweat. Time and time again, I tried to stop the nightmares, but they just kept coming. In those days, I had never heard of PTSD or survivor's guilt. Back then, therapy wasn't on my radar. I never received any help of that type, and it was a long, slow process of working through the trauma. Little did I know that a pattern for my recovery process was being established—just me and God. Complete reliance on God would prove again and again to provide me the absolute best care possible.

It took two years, but when the NTSB finished reconstructing the crash, it was determined that our left wing clipped several trees eighty feet above the ground. This impact spun the plane left toward a massive mausoleum that stood in the middle of a cemetery. It was a concrete and marble memorial, over one hundred feet tall, fifty feet by fifty feet wide, capped with a mosaic dome. (In my previous book *Flight To Heaven,* it was stated as 75 feet tall. But since the writing of that account, the blueprints and experts have corrected that height to closer to 120 feet.) It was massive. Immovable. This gorgeous architectural structure was built in 1924 and named "Portal of the Folded Wings." It was erected in memory of dead aviators.

The Navajo aircraft struck the mausoleum only five feet from the top of its brightly tiled domed cap. The report from the NTSB said we collided at an official impact speed of 135 miles per hour. Of course, the concrete and marble structure provided no give; we came to a sudden and complete stop.

Following the high-speed collision, our airplane shattered into thousands of pieces. The cockpit exploded, leaving no protection for the pilots. As if shot from a cannon, our bodies catapulted through the air, then free-fell seven stories to the ground.

Even this experience became a ghostly memory in dream after dream. I'd awaken in a sweat with my body dropping through some strange space. Frantically, instinctively, whirling my arms in a futile attempt to upright myself as I held my breath, waiting for the inevitable bone-crushing strike with the ground.

Some of what happened next I learned from the written accident reports and eyewitness testimony. My lifeless body was found compressed in the mangled cockpit instrument panel that was lying at the base of the Portal of the Folded Wings.

My body had been impaled in multiple places with metal, Plexiglas, and wood shrapnel from the crash. The entire scene, including all three bodies, was doused in volatile 100-octane aviation fuel.

OUT OF BODY

Rising over the wreckage, I hovered about fifteen feet above the ground. Like a silent observer, I was trying to grasp my new reality. At first, I didn't understand it. Questions swirled through my mind. *Where am I? What is this? Who are these people?*

My focus gravitated toward the disfigured bodies below of three men lying near the base of the building, within a few feet of each other.

The first body looked a little like Gene, the man I'd met less than an hour earlier. I barely recognized him. He was dead, having sustained enormous damage. Let me just say that his face had been erased. *I don't understand. What's happening?*

I recoiled when I looked at the second motionless body. It was Chuck—my flight instructor, friend, and mentor. *No, no, no! This can't be real!*

In disbelief, I turned my attention to the third body lying motionless, bloodied, crushed into the mangled instrument panel only a few feet from Chuck. He was a young man dressed in gray slacks and a white pilot shirt. His face was distorted, but even with the disfigured face, there could be no doubt. The body of the lifeless young man below was mine.

> For the things which are seen are temporary, but the things which are not seen are eternal (2 Corinthians 4:18).

As I think back to my reaction upon first seeing my body, I'm still amazed. Highly disfigured and damaged, I was almost beyond recognition. And yet, surprisingly, I remained relatively calm. I do remember having feelings of sadness, mainly because my young life was over so suddenly, so abruptly.

EXISTING IN TWO PLACES

How could I be in two places at the same time? It was this realization at that moment that changed everything. Instantly, I understood who I *really* was. A lightning bolt of revelation filled my mind and penetrated my heart. It was then and there that I understood. Although the damaged body below was mine, it wasn't me. *I'm not a body. I'm spirit.*

My soul was also connected to my spirit and was intact. The soul—my mind, my will, and my emotions—was working. In fact, better than ever. Only my physical body had been discarded. My body was more or less like a car, taking me where I wanted to go on earth. Now I was out of it, and it was no longer needed.

I was very curious about everything around me, yet I felt no panic or worry. Outside of my body, I began taking in the scene from an entirely new point of view. My perspective of this world, and indeed the earth and entire universe, had shifted dramatically and permanently. Not only that, but suddenly I felt like I was experiencing other dimensions. There were at least a dozen dimensions that I became aware of, and at this point of my journey anyway, I didn't understand much of anything, at least not yet.

AT THE CRASH SITE

Everything was eerily quiet and still, except for the bank checks floating down from above, like falling leaves in slow motion. Then I remembered. Bank checks were the cargo our plane was carrying. I reached my hand out to catch one, but it passed right through.

From my suspended state in spirit form, I sensed a disconnect between the spirit realm and the physical. As a test, I tapped my fingers together to see if they would touch. They did. I reached to touch my arm. I could feel it. It felt normal. I rubbed it gently with my other hand and learned my new spiritual body had substance, at least to me.

I tried several tests and discovered that, although I could feel my new form, I couldn't interface with things that were physical on earth. I was very much alive but was existing inside a different dimension, separate from the physical realm. I couldn't feel or touch the checks as they drifted down. I couldn't feel my damaged physical body or the instrument panel of the cockpit that it laid against.

Yet strangely, I felt vibrantly alive in my new state. In fact, I felt far more alive than before the crash. But there were new rules governing how things worked in this spirit realm that I was just beginning to understand.

> *For we who are in this tent groan, being burdened, not because we want to be unclothed, but further clothed, that mortality may be swallowed up by life* (2 Corinthians 5:4).

SPIRIT, SOUL, AND BODY

It suddenly made perfect sense that my body is not who I am. My spirit is the *real* me. My earthly body is restricted to this earth and the physical dimension, but my spirit and soul are eternal. I am an *eternal* being made in the image of God. In my out-of-body state, it all made perfect sense. And after more than fifty years of scrutiny, it makes perfect sense to me now.

At the time, it seemed so natural to try to reconnect with my physical body, which still lay motionless below. It used to *belong* to me. I tried to touch my damaged body but was not able to connect. Just as with the paper checks, my hand passed right through. In my spiritual state of existence, nothing of this world had substance.

Something else had changed, and it too was strange. I could hear sounds but only in muffled tones. Sounds were not normal. It was as if my ears were filled with dense cotton. Later, this would change dramatically, but I'll save telling you about that for the right time.

Still hovering over the crash site, I heard the distinct sounds of sirens getting louder. Earthly help was on the way. Two men wearing military uniforms were watching from a safe distance from the street. Then I noticed three men running toward the crash site from the nearby Lockheed Aircraft building. They were the first on the scene. They began a quick inspection of the three pilots in the field of debris. My face and head were covered in blood, but later I found out that one of the witnesses said there was no blood flow. This is one of the reasons he believed all three of us were dead. Another one shouted, "They're dead, all dead. Get back! There's fuel everywhere."

Moments earlier, we had taken off with both fuel tanks topped off, so there was high-octane aviation fuel *everywhere*. To make matters worse, two very hot engines lay on the ground in the middle of the fuel-soaked scene with fumes wafting throughout the area. The Lockheed men were afraid they'd be engulfed in flames at any moment.

A picture of this exact scene was taken by the well-known professional photographer, Harold Moresby of Channel Five news in Los Angeles. He snapped the amazing photo from his hovering helicopter just minutes after the crash. Smoke was seen still rising from one of the hot engines, and the witnesses said in their statements that they were certain a large fire was imminent. The NTSB official report would later state that it was incredible and highly unusual that there was no fire.

Many have said that God performed a miracle by keeping fire from igniting the scene. The Burbank Fire Department attributed the lack of fire to their quick response and the spraying of fire retardant onto the crash site. Of course, they would claim this, but it took more than ten minutes for them to arrive. It is nothing short of a miracle that there wasn't an explosive ball of flames engulfing the entire scene. You should know that two years later, the final NTSB report indicated that both engines were operating at full power right up until impact. RPM indicators, oil pressure gauges, and damage to the propellers all indicated that there was no engine failure of any kind. In fact, the engines were straining at high manifold pressure (high power).

Years later, I became an aviation safety counselor and Federal Aviation Administration (FAA) examiner. I visited almost a hundred crash sights, and fire was a part of almost all of them. I have met survivors of airplane crashes who were severely burned, yet the crash they were involved in had less fuel and a less flammable environment than ours. I will always credit God's mercy over me because of the daily prayers of my parents and grandparents.

EMERGENCY VEHICLES

Within a few moments, emergency vehicles descended on the scene. The screaming siren of an ambulance suddenly went silent as it pulled to a stop, and two paramedics blasted out the back door. I moved slowly above the wreckage, looking down, watching the flurry of activity. No one knew I was there.

Somehow I stayed near my dead body. Though I wasn't panicked about the situation, still I consistently chose to remain close to the nineteen-year-old, lifeless, messed-up body of Dale Russell Black.

> *Remember your Creator before the silver cord is loosed.... Then the dust will return to the earth as it was, and the spirit will return to God who gave it* (Ecclesiastes 12:6-7).

TRAVERSING THE SPIRITUAL DIMENSION

In the years following, I have often wondered how exactly I moved about during this time out of my body. Whatever I was doing didn't seem the least bit strange. I know that I moved; that was obvious. But how? It didn't feel like I exerted any effort or that I used muscles or ligaments. I didn't feel my feet, toes, or ankles move. I felt none of the forces generally associated with movement on earth, yet I moved. I just moved.

Months after the crash, I continued to contemplate many things about Heaven and my time in the spiritual dimension, including how I moved around following the crash. I am now convinced that all movement in the spiritual dimension is controlled by thought or desire, but not simply by thought. It's by thoughts of words and images.

I believe it is thinking *words* or thinking in *pictures* that allows movement in the spiritual realm. I'm not talking about *speaking* words out loud but *thinking* them, and turning those thoughts into expectation. Focused desire of the heart creates movement. In that dimension, if I desired and imagined going somewhere, then I went there. If I pictured in my mind and desired in my heart something specific, then my spirit responded to accomplish it. I believe that movement in Heaven is controlled not just by thought as others have declared but more precisely by inner images and articulate desires of the heart.

THE THIRD PARAMEDIC

Back inside the boundaries of Valhalla Memorial Park, next to the gigantic Portal of the Folded Wings Shrine to Aviation, the ambulance driver remained inside the vehicle. The second and third paramedics began checking the victims of the terrible crash for signs of life.

Gene lay motionless, still strapped to the captain's chair. There was no doubt. Gene was dead. The third paramedic found me, as I mentioned earlier, smashed into the instrument panel. He began

CPR. Witnesses said he did chest compressions and mouth-to-mouth resuscitation. He was calm, patient, and professional.

Bless this man's heart. He worked on me as if I were one of his own family members. It seemed as if he were helping me *personally*.

My *spirit* continued to watch the paramedic conduct CPR. At times I was hovering just a few feet above my body, and at other times I was ten or even fifteen feet above the ground. I wondered why this man was working so hard to resuscitate me. *I've never felt more alive.*

Before the crash, I had it all mixed up. My perception of truth was upside down and reversed. But at that moment, when I saw three dead pilots—one of whom was me—I finally could understand things as they truly *are*.

Once I experienced this revolutionary revelation, everything I knew shifted, and I have remained transformed to this day. I believe this is what happens to everyone who *actually* dies. I'm not talking about the many stories of people who claim to have died. I'm describing only those who were *clinically* dead. Suddenly, the dead realize that they too are a spirit, they have a soul, and they no longer live in a body.

Let's get back to the crash site. Just moments after the impact with the one hundred foot tall mausoleum and the subsequent fall to the ground, I continued observing the scene below. I felt absolutely no pain.

Then—instantly—everything changed. Again!

In less time than the blink of an eye, I was back inside my mangled body. An explosion of pain hit me like a bolt of lightning. It felt like a blast of hot electricity shot through every cell of my body. The pain was excruciating, and at that moment, I much preferred death. *God, please! Let me pass out or die.*

According to the reports, I did both.

CHAPTER 10

THE HORRORS OF HELL

And do not fear those who kill the body but cannot kill the soul. But rather fear Him who is able to destroy both soul and body in hell.
                                                                —MATTHEW 10:28

Reportedly, I was resuscitated at the scene. The ambulance accelerated out of Valhalla Memorial Park with the bodies of Chuck and me. We sped through early morning traffic along the streets of Burbank toward the emergency room of nearby St. Joseph's Hospital. Paramedics call this "the ride." In my case, it wasn't so much a *ride*. It was more of a *chase*.

CONNECTED TO MY BODY

During our trip to the hospital, I again separated from my body and followed slightly above and behind the ambulance. I had little to no spatial orientation and didn't think about being in Burbank or even that I'd been in an airplane crash. The fact that we were heading to a hospital was irrelevant to me. My only thoughts were regarding two souls—Chuck and me. Looking through the rear windows at our bodies, for the first time since the accident

I thought about eternity. Eternity was now very real. In fact, I realized that I was *already* in eternity. The odd realization was that the paramedics were too, since human spirits are eternal and never die.

What will happen to Chuck? What will happen to me? What's going to happen next? Where will we go?

Even though I was outside the fast-moving ambulance, I could clearly see the paramedic inside actively working on my body. It was puzzling to be following the speeding vehicle. Somehow I knew to stay close to my body as I effortlessly chased behind. I didn't understand how the "out-of-body" stuff worked back then, but I do remember that I still felt connected to my body, even when I wasn't inside of it. I don't mean to imply that I was linked to my body physically, at least I couldn't *see* a connection—but I certainly *felt* one. Some strong and compelling force prompted me to remain close, even though at times we must have been moving greater than fifty miles per hour.

During the chase and without warning, I slammed back into my body, instantly assaulted by the agonizing pain—pain more intense than I had ever imagined was possible to endure. The moments of excruciating awareness seemed to last a lifetime. Then once again, I separated from my body, and the agony instantly vanished. Gratefully, with the pain gone, I was left to watch the moving scenes unfold in relative peace.

My last recollection of this chase was from outside the ambulance, looking through the glass at two bloodied bodies strapped to gurneys, Chuck and me, motionless.

No survivors. Obviously, there are no survivors.

EMERGENCY ROOM

The ambulance came to a halt in front of the emergency doors at St. Joseph's Hospital. It was 6:56 a.m. on July 18, 1969.

I approached the hospital doors, traveling alongside my body, which was being transported on a wheeled gurney. I remember seeing bold red lights and hearing muffled sounds of activity as we exploded through the doors of the emergency entrance. The gurney was instantly surrounded by personnel who rushed my body through hallways. I could hear the scuffing sounds of wheels and shoes racing over linoleum.

Lights moved past in a blur. Occasionally, a concerned face looked down into my face. *Hey, guys. Hello. I'm not there. I'm up here.*

We came to an abrupt stop in a large room where they transferred me from a blue gurney onto a sturdy table with a thin pad. Peering down, I noticed a nurse quickly cutting off my gray slacks and white shirt, which were torn to shreds and soaked in blood and fuel. Others were connecting my broken body to monitors and setting an IV. Though I knew it was *my* body that was so badly disfigured and damaged, I still wasn't panicked. I continued to remain more curious than anything else.

As my clothes were removed, I couldn't help but notice the visible damage. Aircraft debris was sticking out of my head and limbs. My grossly disfigured face had long deep cuts, too many to count. My chin was nearly severed from my face, and a huge gash sliced across my forehead, extending down through the middle of the right eye. My nose was a bloodied mess. It seemed apparent that almost every bone was broken, contributing to my disfigurement.

A man I had not seen before quietly entered the room. He was a distinguished gray-haired doctor who showed no sign of emotion as he began inspecting his new patient. I watched from above as he explored my disfigured face and head, then stoically turned to study the monitors. His mannerisms and countenance exuded a show of power and command. It seemed clear that he was in control of the room and every person in it.

Though only a few feet above the commotion, no one seemed to notice I was even present.

"Give me the paddles," the doctor ordered.

That was my introduction to Dr. Homer Graham, a man who would have a powerful influence on my survival and my life afterward. As it turned out, my survival would in turn have a powerful influence on his life as well.

INVISIBLE ME

Hovering near the end of the table, just above my feet and slightly below the acoustical ceiling, I could see the entire room. A variety of gleaming stainless-steel instruments lay in neat rows on white sterile napkins, poised and waiting to be put to use.

As the trauma team worked diligently on my body, I still felt surprisingly detached and unaffected by what I saw. It was a schizophrenic sensation, being in two places at the same time. The most real part of me was hovering above, suspended over the discarded physical part of me on the table below.

I felt for my body much like I did for, say, my senior year varsity jacket. I knew it was mine, and I was attached—even proud of it. But I didn't *need* it to be me. Or like my car...I liked my

MGB convertible. Well, okay, I *loved* it. But my car was simply an *instrument* that took me places I wanted to go.

In like manner, my body is the physical structure for my spirit and soul. It is the link to my human experience. It takes me places—houses my spirit and soul during my earth life. This truth was evident to me immediately upon leaving my body at the scene of the crash. I am something eternal, much greater than the physical part of me.

No longer was I afraid of death. I realized that death is nothing more than a transfer from one dimension to another. Death isn't the end of anything. We continue living but without the earthly garment that limits us to the physical realm. There is only one concern every person should have about death—*where* will they go when they die?

> *For God so loved the world that He gave His only begotten Son, that whoever believes in Him should not perish but have everlasting life* (John 3:16).

In the out-of-body dimension, new sensations are greatly magnified and enhanced. The sensations I was experiencing were far deeper and more profound than any feelings I had ever experienced in my life previously. I found colors, for example, to be—how shall I say it? *Super enhanced.* Colors were prominent and striking. Not just some colors. *Any* color. Color suddenly became highly *important* to me.

Worldly matters were now insignificant. From my new eternal perspective, I no longer cared whether I could fly airplanes or be a commercial airline pilot. Countries, governments, and politics didn't matter anymore. It was not important that man was about to set foot on the moon or what kind of car I drove. At that point, only eternal things mattered. And those things continue to matter to me now.

> *And the world is passing away, and the lust of it; but he who does the will of God abides forever* (1 John 2:17).

I was very aware of my surroundings, but no one seemed aware of me. The medical professionals were oblivious to my presence. They paid no attention to the *real* Dale Black. Yet I was right there, only two or three feet away, watching with startling clarity.

Suddenly, there was a huge commotion in the next room that grabbed all my attention. It drew me, pulling on my spirit and soul with a heaviness I had never known before.

GLIMPSE OF HELL

I would give anything to report that what I'm about to tell you never happened. I really mean that. I still can't talk or even write about this experience without tears coming to my eyes. These are tears of heartache. It was and still is the most terrible and horrifying event that I have ever experienced in my life.

There are a few reasons I'm reluctant to share this. First, because of its horrific nature. No one wants to relive a horrible experience. Second, it can't be proved. I prefer sharing things that are solid, verifiable, and scientifically provable. Third, my nature is to protect the feelings of my friend's family. Nevertheless, I believe in my heart that God wants me to tell you this part of the story. It has been over fifty years, giving more than enough time for Chuck's children to become adults and make their own assessment of these events. Yet, just as with everything that took place in the spiritual realm, this event remains as vivid and powerful as if it occurred a moment ago. Let me tell you what happened.

Suspended above my body in the emergency room, my attention fixed on the medical personnel scurrying in and out of the adjacent room—like bees around a poked hive. Something big was happening. I could see the reactions and *feel* an increasing, overwhelming dread. I strained to see what was causing the pandemonium, but my view was blocked by a partition of thick gray curtains I couldn't see through or over.

The voices coming from behind the barrier were tense but garbled, and I was unable to discern what was being said. My hearing was the only one of my senses to have become more diminished in my out-of-body state. Every other sense was heightened and more sensitive. But nothing was as strong as my new awareness. I could sense emotions, perceive conditions, and feel things more deeply. It's odd what mattered and what didn't. It was almost the reverse of what we deal with in normal earthly life.

Something of extreme urgency assaulted me at my core—deep in my heart. There was an intensity and overwhelming agitation in the hospital's atmosphere. I could focus on nothing else. Even the light seemed to be sucked out of the room as my anxiety grew stronger.

Like a pounding surf, wave after wave of heartbreaking anguish crashed over me. Although I didn't yet know what was happening to the person in the adjacent room, I did know that it was *catastrophic*.

I was sensing a life and death struggle—but worse. Much worse. Worse than physical death by far. Infinitely worse! A battle raged, a battle pertaining to Heaven and hell. And it was far more crucial than a struggle for mere physical life. Someone's eternal destination was at stake. In the next moments, it became clear to me that the verdict had already been rendered. It was too late to change it. The outcome had been determined.

A palpable heaviness filled the atmosphere as the area grew darker. The doctors and nurses were oblivious to what was happening as I quickly realized these changes were occurring in the same dimension in which I existed—the spiritual realm, the truest dimension of reality.

My senses were by far the strongest aspect of what I witnessed next. These were not physical senses like on earth. I would describe my new awareness more accurately as *spiritual discernment*. With this new ability to perceive things, in what I now call the *first dimension*, I watched as evil spirits entered the adjacent space. They slithered through space like snakes through grass, slowing occasionally, as if listening for something. They were several in number, though I couldn't determine exactly how many. They looked somewhat human in shape, with limbs and appendages, but moved in ways no human could. It reminded me of a pack of wild dogs pursuing prey, but in slow motion. They blended into the darkness that seemed to grow thicker with each millisecond. I began to feel like I was choking, as if my throat were closing, a strange reaction, given that I wasn't even physically breathing. That's how strong these sensations were.

The worst part was the sheer terror that filled the atmosphere. It was suffocating. These entities were demonic. Though I didn't label them as such at the time, I certainly knew they were evil. They soon found the soul they were seeking in the adjacent room. Their target was a person unidentifiable to me. I sensed their victim struggle, resisting, terrified. This person was a spirit, much like me. I could sense what no one else in the room could see, as this soul was taken against its will, kicking and screaming, trying to get free. Obviously, it was too late. This person no longer had a choice—and no adequate power to resist.

> *Wide is the gate and broad is the way that leads to destruction, and there are many who go in by it. Because narrow is the gate and difficult is the way which leads to life, and there are few who find it* (Matthew 7:13-14).

CHAPTER 11

MY FLIGHT TO HEAVEN

I am the resurrection and the life. He who believes in
Me, though he may die, he shall live.
—John 11:25

FLASH-FORWARD—1970—DR. HOMER GRAHAM'S OFFICE

Almost a year after the crash, while seeking information from
Dr. Graham—the doctor who treated me in the emergency room
on the day of the crash—my worst nightmare was confirmed. I
pressed him for details about who was in the space next to me in
the hospital when I had first arrived. Dr. Graham confided that
in fact it was Chuck Burns who died in the adjacent room that
day. In the months following the crash, I had often wondered if it
could have been Chuck behind the curtain, but I always pushed
the thoughts away, unable to face that possibility as fact.

Finally, I knew. It was Chuck who had struggled with the
terrifying evil forces that had been present. I believe my friend
and aviation mentor was taken to hell by the demonic forces I
witnessed that morning in the hospital. But the story doesn't
end there. I also believe that God allowed me to experience that
event so I could warn others. That awful experience altered my

perspective forever. As I mentioned previously, it was the most horrifying experience of my life. God is real—I know that for sure. But satan is also real. And there is an eternal battle raging for every soul on planet Earth, including yours.

Chuck was a man I had grown to care about, respect, and admire. We had spent a lot of time together—had a lot of conversations while flying. At that time in my life, I already understood the Bible's teaching that Jesus was the only way to eternal life with God in Heaven. I had accepted Jesus into my life as a youth. Yet I said nothing to Chuck. Not once did I utter a word about God or discuss anything spiritual. I was in no hurry. I thought we had a lifetime ahead of us. I'm not blaming myself for Chuck's spiritual condition, yet I live with leftover guilt due to my omission in being a witness to the truth.

The horror of what happened to my dear friend caused such deep sorrow that there are not strong enough words to describe it. I think about Chuck every day. While separated from my body, I felt every emotion at a level impossible to experience in the physical dimension. My senses were heightened, unfiltered, and overwhelming. That intensity of the bone-chilling fear isn't possible to contain in the human experience. I felt pure spiritual destruction and loss, surpassing all the combined terror I had ever felt in my life.

When I recall that event, it still takes my breath away. And the memory of Chuck's struggle in death causes me to think about eternity and the spiritual condition of each person in the entire human population. This too, I think about every day.

Multitudes, multitudes in the valley of decision! For the day of the Lord is near in the valley of decision (Joel 3:14).

SUDDEN LIFE REVIEW

Eventually, the darkness receded from the emergency room as the bone-chilling sounds faded away. I remained hovering over my broken body, watching the medical personnel busy at work. I wondered why they were trying so hard to save me.

There's something else that happened before I left the hospital that you'll want to know about. A series of images began flashing through my mind. But these images extended beyond my mind. They were scenes actually playing out, and it was as if I were a part of them—but only as an observer.

An impressionistic collage of moments of my life replayed in fast succession. While it seemed like each scene lasted only a millisecond, in my new state of being, every detail made itself fully known. However, one event stood out—more focused—as if the review remained longer so that I could fully focus on this single event.

Looking back, I realize why it was important for this event to have been shown to me, especially in light of the horror I had witnessed only moments earlier. The scene took place in a mountain chapel at summer church camp when I was eleven. I was kneeling in front of a wooden cross, and a pastor was kneeling at my side. Speaking softly, he said, "God loved the world so much that He sent His one and only Son, and anyone who believes in Him will have eternal life. Dale, God did *not* send His Son into the world to judge or condemn. Jesus was sent to *save* all who believe in Him."

I observed the image play out. There I was, kneeling and nodding, smiling. Following the pastor's instructions, I watched as the young me bowed my head while the pastor led me in prayer to receive Jesus. While I was watching, a brilliant light grew around the young me as I prayed. I was enveloped by God's glowing presence. To this day, I still remember the event with clarity.

Following this scene, like an old movie, I saw quick cuts of various experiences throughout my life as I grew older. The light and glow around me became progressively dimmer as I became more selfish and prideful. These images ended with the unmistakable crash of a twin-engine airplane splintering into ten-thousand pieces as it collided with a huge marble mausoleum. This final scene was swallowed up by an immense light.

And the dead were judged according to their works, by the things which were written in the books (Revelation 20:12).

When the brilliant light melded into the bright lights of the emergency room, a stark realization hit me. I was no longer the innocent, tenderhearted boy I had just observed in the chapel. I had become arrogant and self-centered—someone who loved a lot of things about living but barely concerned himself any longer with the things that God cared about.

My life had gradually become all about me. It was about *my* life. *My* vocation. *My* hopes. *My* dreams. It was also about being wealthy and respected and in control. Immediately, I felt shame wash through me. A heavy sensation of sadness and grief again weighed me down. For a moment, I felt like the weight of those feelings would pull me through the same floor that I was hovering above.

Moments later, the heaviness left. I felt light again, like a helium balloon being released. My speed slowly increased as I moved out of the room, down the hallway, going faster as the walls dissolved into a long, brightly lit corridor. I felt a gentle wind, and I began moving effortlessly into the corridor of light. There was the sense of a gentle pulling. An invisible force was drawing me like a paperclip toward a powerful magnet.

Surprise gave way to anticipation as I began to glide higher and away from my body. Deep down inside, I began to sense something. Anticipation was building—anticipation of something wondrous.

As I try to explain this to you, keep in mind that my physical body was still in the hospital. I was traveling and experiencing all of this with my spirit and soul in a different type of body. Still, I felt complete—like nothing was missing. I had arms and legs, eyes to see and ears to hear. You may wish to know that I felt the same size and as if I had the same *reach* as my physical body. But in my new state, I clearly had some new and awesome capabilities.

SPACE FLIGHT

Once free from St. Joseph's Hospital, my speed rapidly increased as I was pulled upward until the hospital and the city of Burbank itself completely vanished from view. I went from merely moving gently forward, to racing at breakneck speed into what looked like deep outer space. Day turned to night. I had no control of my speed or direction, yet it was clear that I was being guided with some purpose. The emergency room, my broken body, even the terror of what I had experienced were no longer in my thoughts. My entire being was focused on the incredible pinpoint of light ahead that was growing in size and beauty as my unimaginable speed continued to increase.

My course was lit by a beam of light emanating from my chest—like a searchlight directing my journey—stretching out in front of me as far as I could see. I sped through this narrow pathway, surrounded by darkness but safely ensconced within the corridor of brilliant light.

Though I traveled very quickly, I saw millions of small spheres of light constantly zooming past. The speed at which I traveled doesn't make earthly sense and was beyond anything we can relate to in the physical realm on earth. Even moving at those blinding speeds, I felt no discomfort. In fact, there wasn't anything to make me *feel* like I was moving. There was no pain or G-forces. I didn't feel queasy or have the customary ear-popping like on earth.

Even then, I didn't feel apprehensive. I had no serious concerns. All I had were simple questions. *What is happening? Where am I going? What's going to happen next?*

The beam of light emanating from me was gradually overpowered by a thick pure light that I was moving toward. Growing in size and brilliance as I drew nearer, this intoxicating light expanded upward and outward in such massive proportion that it was difficult to comprehend. The center of the light was the whitest of whites I had ever seen. I didn't know that white could be so pure and clean and perfect. I had always thought of white as being without color. However, this white contained within it every color imaginable, yet it was still pure white brilliance.

The light beams emanating from this central source that lay ahead gradually became yellow-white and then golden. Eventually, everything was bathed in rich golden hues. The light's properties were unlike any type of light I had ever seen. It was breathtaking, and I will never think of light the same way again. I was experiencing light in a way I had never imagined. It behaved like a living substance.

In truth, the light of Heaven *is* alive. It is a living substance brighter than the sun. My eyes should have been burned away by the intensity of it, but instead, I was drawn into the holy brightness like a moth to the flame. I wish I had more ability to describe this glorious light. I have tried often since I returned but have always lacked the words. But here I go, trying again.

It still amazes me how every aspect of Heaven is so significant—down to the smallest things. The light embodied something divine and perfect; I was sure of that.

ANGELIC GUIDES

As I was traveling toward the brilliant light, which was still far in the distance, I became aware that I was being accompanied by two angelic guides. These companions were slightly behind me and one on each side. I could almost see both at the same time, due to my greatly enhanced peripheral vision. With only a slight turn to the left or right, these magnificent angels came into view. Each one was wrapped in a golden, glowing aura that resonated from their bodies. Light radiated from their glorious faces, which expressed great delight at escorting me. I was enthralled with how jubilant they appeared. Love seemed to radiate from these angelic beings, and I basked in the sensation of this unifying love. I felt safe and at peace in their presence.

For He shall give His angels charge over you, to keep you in all your ways (Psalm 91:11).

Both angels were larger than I was and appeared masculine and human-like, yet not male or female. They were clothed in long, seamless white garments with silver threads woven through the fabric and had a golden band circling their waist. Their hair, perfectly trimmed, appeared as shiny brass.

Though the angels had large wings, they didn't flap like birds on earth. Throughout my time in Heaven, I observed many different angels, some with wings and some apparently without. Yet I noticed that, when the wings were folded against their bodies, they fit so perfectly that they would almost disappear. At other times, they would open and were astonishing.

The angels' wings seemed to connect to their inner heart. Their wings often seemed to display emotion by their positioning and movement. When they praised God, for example, their wings moved in beautiful gyrations or stretched upward in adoration. It was another one of the beauties of God's creation.

Praise Him, all His angels; praise Him, all His hosts! (Psalm 148:2).

CHAPTER 12

THE CELESTIAL CITY

*The city had no need of the sun or of the moon to shine
in it, for the glory of God illuminated it. The Lamb is its
light.*

—Revelation 21:23

Traveling at unimaginable speed through deep outer space, I was
being directed by two angelic escorts toward a brilliant pinpoint
of light ahead in the far distance. Night gradually became day as
the celestial skyline of a magnificent golden city began to reveal
itself from the center of the brilliant light. As the light traveled
outward from its center, it gradually changed from white to yellow
to light gold, then to a rich, deep, lavish gold. It was mesmerizing.

The city was of unimaginable size and grandeur, eventually
filling the entire horizon in all directions as far as I could see. On
earth, as a professional jet captain, I've been privileged to travel
the globe and visit many of the world's major cities. But never
have I seen a metropolis that could even remotely compare with
the colossal size of the Celestial City. Thick, pure, white light
radiated outward for miles and miles in every direction.

Like an airplane on final approach, my speed began to slow until we were gently gliding above a gorgeous and colorful countryside. At this point in my journey, I was not in control of when or where I moved. I didn't question how I traveled and felt no concern whatsoever. In fact, never—in my entire life—have I felt more at peace.

As I drew nearer to the glorious landscape beneath me, I became increasingly enraptured by everything I encountered. Sounds of indescribable music filled the atmosphere. Amazing new colors swirled in sync with the melodies, overflowing the land with textures and vibrations I could literally *feel*.

CITY OF GOD

Even though the city was still far, far in the distance, its grandeur took my breath away. This was a city without a visible end. The massive metropolis was securely surrounded by a huge and colorful wall, which wrapped the city as if in a comforting embrace.

From my elevated vantage point, I could see over the impressive barrier into the city. The spectacular beauty I encountered with my first glimpse beyond the wall only fueled my intense desire to enter.

On the other side of the enormous wall, lush gardens with striking colors encircled spectacular structures. It was architectural perfection. It appeared to me as if the city had been designed to be viewed from above. From my suspended vantage point, it was a masterpiece.

Positioned throughout the city were many *townships*. This is the word I've chosen to use because these communities looked like small, happy, colorful towns. Together, they made up the colossal city. Each township from my elevated view was settled within a park-like setting with colorful gardens, fountains, lakes, and streams. Beautiful homes of various sizes and designs were everywhere. And although I could see many communities, nothing looked crowded.

Each township was amazingly unique and none less attractive than another. They made up a masterfully planned community, each independently exceptional, yet strategically part of the whole.

MINISTRY OF MUSIC

It started with gentle musical sounds accompanied by the delicate ringing of an assortment of bells, reminding me of delightful wind chimes. I've heard many wind chimes on earth that are not pleasant—at least not to me. But this was the most joyful and enticing of any sound I'd ever experienced.

Faintly at first, and then with more volume, I heard the most magnificent and graceful vocal and instrumental music I'd ever encountered—as if thousands of choirs and orchestras had gathered and prepared a glorious presentation. There were so many harmonies—each perfectly balanced. Music was suddenly coming from, well, everywhere. Divine sounds played from a source I couldn't identify.

On earth, when I hear music or a loud sound, like others, I instinctively turn my head toward the source. But this lovely music was just there—everywhere. And keep in mind, I didn't have physical ears—at least I don't think I did. My body was still on earth, but in this celestial place, I was hearing heavenly, divine music with spiritual ears—sounds so perfect and complete that words are unable to describe it. Take the range, for example. I heard octaves and notes that extended well beyond what is physically possible on earth. That's part of the reason it's so difficult to describe. The music was more than audible. It seemed… alive. It had *substance* and *power.* It pulsated with *life.* And it imparted *love.*

I heard voices singing, too many to number. Not only voices but also diverse kinds of instruments—many I had never heard before.

There is still so much I don't understand about the music in Heaven, so much I'd love to know more about. But of one thing I am certain—all music, including all the voices and instruments, all sounds, pointed toward one being: God. All were worshipping the one true, living God—the Creator of all things.

Music is a language of expression, and in Heaven, it seemed to be the language that ministered to all at the deepest levels. It was a force—a powerful spiritual force, a conduit of entry into God's presence.

I was fascinated as I watched the colors and light respond to the music. As I mentioned previously, light was in everything, and within the light was every imaginable color in countless hues and shades. The light and colors moved and pulsed with each note and vibration, appearing to sway in the atmosphere. They made me think of the Northern Lights and what it would be like to walk through those gyrating colors while a world-class symphony played its best arrangement. As wonderful as that would be on earth, it would appear a sloppy and poor imitation of Heaven's musical light show. It wasn't really a show…it was an *experience.* And a ministry.

> *Praise the Lord! Praise God in His sanctuary; praise Him in His mighty firmament!* (Psalm 150:1).

Praise Him with the sound of the trumpet; praise Him with the lute and harp! Praise Him with the timbrel and dance; praise Him with stringed instruments and flutes! Praise Him with loud cymbals; praise Him with clashing cymbals! (Psalm 150:5).

When I returned from Heaven, I had a deep love and longing for Heaven's music. Only in rare and wonderful moments here on earth have I had even a small taste of that glorious experience.

LIGHT, LIFE, AND LOVE

When I first arrived in Heaven's countryside, I noticed the most brilliant light still in the far distance. This intense light was brighter than the sun, but it didn't hurt my eyes to look at it. It was coming from behind the wall, originating from somewhere near the center of the massive city. From this colossal light source, bright beams of what looked like *liquid* light erupted gracefully into the sky, arching hundreds of miles upward and outward alongside countless others that were being birthed every second. This created a dazzling display, a sight I might compare to looking at our sun's enormous solar flares while standing on the sun's surface! The light's radiance and glory were simply not containable. The light blanketed the entire heavenly atmosphere and everyone and everything in it.

In Heaven, light has substance. It does not dissipate at the end of its journey. Instead, it is absorbed gratefully by everyone and everything it touches. And it touches everything. With its touch, the light fills, satisfies, and rejuvenates with life, energy, and love. Within it is life—God's life. Light has within it love—perfect, pure, and complete love.

Maybe I can best describe it as *indescribable*.

In Him was life, and the life was the light of men (John 1:4).

God is light and in Him is no darkness at all (1 John 1:5).

For God is love (1 John 4:8).

The Celestial City is filled with light, light as plentiful as air is to us on earth. All are ministered to by the light, and all in turn reflect the light—not a reflection *off of* but *through*.

Understanding the light, life, and love in Heaven is fundamental to being in Heaven. From Heaven's center—the throne room of God—beams of soft, living light cascade out to every part of Heaven without ceasing. It is the very essence of God's presence, imparting its benefits to all. Light is absorbed by everything and released again without diminishing—only refracting into more colors and shades of white. It radiates through the grass, the trees, the animals, and the people—everything and everyone that exists in Heaven is a conduit of the light.

Bear with me. I know I've already talked at length about the light, but how am I supposed to explain something so revolutionary and radical—something that has completely transformed my understanding of creation, earth, Heaven, and Almighty God? Experiencing the light in Heaven turned my reality on earth inside out and upside down. How could anyone be the same after being touched by this light?

Forty years after the experience, when I finally felt the urging of God to tell my wife about Heaven, one of the things I found myself repeating to her was the symbiotic relationship between

Heaven's light and God's love and life. All three are so connected and intertwined; they are as one. Paula would listen intently, trying to grasp my explanation, but I could tell she didn't *get* it. To me, this was one of the most amazing truths I experienced while in Heaven—*so how could she not get it?* I attributed her lack of understanding to my inadequate explanation of such a revolutionary and spiritual reality. But as hard as I tried, it was to no avail. One day, this changed. As she describes it now, in answer to her prayers, the Holy Spirit *opened her mind* to understand what I'd repeatedly tried to explain. She finally *got* it. Today, she continues to tell me and others that this understanding of Heaven's light containing life and love has changed her in deep, profound, and meaningful ways.

Now that I've tried to explain Heaven's light, let's consider the attributes of what is in the light—life and love!

Within the light is life. As the light touched me, I was infused with life, energy, strength—the very life of God. I felt as though I could run without ceasing, climb the highest mountain without effort, or accomplish whatever was asked of me without feeling diminished in the least.

I noticed that as the light touched the flowers, trees, animals, water—everything—it ministered eternal, unending life. That is why not a single flower wilts, or a blade of grass dies, or any person ages in Heaven. All are continually being renewed by the life of God from within the light that fills all of Heaven.

As the light permeated the massive wall of the city, it refracted through the stones, creating a rainbow of color. At that moment, it was the most glorious thing I had ever seen—the entire city of Heaven surrounded by a glorious rainbow of light and color, gyrating with life.

The third aspect of the light is love—God's love. Everything in the light is directly imparted from God to all of Heaven. The love that permeated my being was more love than I ever imagined could exist. To say I felt as if I belonged there would be a massive understatement. I was wanted, needed, valued, and priceless to God. He knew me—all my secrets, my regrets, my embarrassments, my sin. Yet I knew He loved me without restriction or hesitation or condition. I was loved completely, more entirely than I could ever hope to be loved. This love from God left no room to feel unworthy of such a gift. The love dominated every other emotion and became the foundation for everything else. Everything God offered or did was rooted in His love for me.

I instantly understood what the Scripture "God is love" actually means. It's not that God is capable of love or has the attribute of being a loving God. He *is* love. It is inseparable from Him. It is *who* He is, *what* He is, and *how* He is. Love *is* God.

THE LIVING WORD

Before visiting Heaven, I had heard and learned many things written in the Bible. I accepted them as the truth because I was taught they are true. Some Scriptures seemed helpful and beneficial, and others seemed difficult to understand and no longer relevant, or outdated. But when I experienced Heaven personally, I quickly realized how truly alive God's Word (the Bible) really is. It is deep and full of revelation. It is eternal, meaning it never becomes obsolete or less needed. It is full of life and revelation, and it never ceases to accomplish whatever it is meant to do.

I returned to life on earth with an understanding of the power of God's living Word. The life of God is in His Word. It is eternal.

Although in Heaven there is no resistance to the manifestation of God's Word, on earth in satan's kingdom, there is nothing but resistance.

Our faith is the detonation that allows the Word of God to release its power. Much like a bomb loaded with explosive ability, it can remain dormant in the confines of the bomb's casing unless the detonation occurs. The detonation that allows God's Word to manifest, is our faith—a firm confidence and trust that God's Word is true and able to accomplish what it is sent to do.

In this fallen world, satan does all he can do to stop the process of detonation because the believer with unshakable faith is satan's greatest enemy and his greatest fear.

HOLINESS

There is another aspect of Heaven that became immediately apparent during the first moments of my arrival. I'm referring to something I still have difficulty explaining, yet it was a powerfully significant part of the entire experience. It cannot be separated from all the wonders I saw and heard and sensed. I'm referring to *holiness*—the overwhelming and powerful sense of God's glorious presence.

On earth when we hear the word *holiness,* we often think of something religious that we don't really understand or feel. Before the airplane crash, holiness certainly didn't have any place in my life. Whenever I'd hear of it, my opinion was that holiness was something uncool and old-fashioned. I mean, who needed holiness? And what is it, really? Going to church was enough holiness for me. But a few minutes in Heaven were all it took for everything to change. And I do mean *everything*. Holiness tops the list. It's even more necessary than the air we breathe on earth. We can't have God without holiness. He is holy. Wherever He is, holiness is there. If we want His presence, it will come with holiness. And the only way on earth we can even remotely be holy is by receiving the shed blood of Jesus in and over our lives.

My dictionary states that *holy* means "connected to God" or "the state of being holy." Whatever that means. This is a gross understatement—offering a two-dimensional definition of something that is infinite. The dictionary goes on to say that holiness can be "a title given to certain religious dignitaries," which is not only a pale description, but in light of Heaven, also entirely wrong. Even the most educated people on earth seem to have no clue as to what real holiness is or the true state of being holy.

> *For thus says the High and Lofty One who inhabits eternity, whose name is Holy; "I dwell in the high and holy place"* (Isaiah 57:15).

By experiencing Heaven, I now can say that *holy* means a lot more than is found in the dictionary or in this world. Holiness radiates out from God, filling the entire land with an intangible yet unmistakable awareness of His presence. *Holy* means righteous. *Holy* means clean. Sinless. Blemish-less. Without error. Without blind spots. Perfection. This dominating sensation came from the source of the light, life, and love. From the One who sits on the throne, the One whose presence fills all of Heaven.

In Heaven, holiness stimulates a response. For me, it created awe, such awe that joyful worship and devotion to God emanated from every part of me. I don't know how. It just did, and not only from me, but also from every being and everything that is a part of Heaven. This sense of holiness that I'm trying to describe caused total devotion in me and, at the same time, unspeakable joy. Yet my response was not mandatory. It wasn't coerced or forced in any way. It was just as I said a moment ago—a free and spontaneous reply to the awesome holiness that originates from the throne.

> *Let them praise Your great and awesome name—He is holy* (Psalm 99:3).

I have been in thousands of church services, meetings, and spiritual events since. Never have I experienced a holy environment on earth that offers more than a *sliver* of a shadow of what exists in Heaven. Never before. Never since. Not even close.

On this side of Heaven, I now *crave* true holiness—God's overwhelming presence. I long for it every day. Holiness is a most awesome aspect of Heaven, and it's everywhere—because God is everywhere and in everything.

We can't earn holiness. We can't buy it or manufacture it. A personal relationship with Jesus is the only way we can become holy in God's eyes and experience God's presence. Jesus is also the only way to Heaven. *All* the people in Heaven are children of God, reborn by the blood of Jesus—which is the single thing that gives them access to Heaven and holiness.

> *Jesus answered, "Most assuredly, I say to you, unless one is born of water and the Spirit, he cannot enter the kingdom of God. That which is born of the flesh is flesh, and that which is born of the Spirit is spirit"* (John 3:5-6).

Because of God's love, He has provided a permanent solution. God longs for every person to enjoy Heaven and spend eternity with Him. We are all in eternity already and will all live forever.

The only question is *where* we will live forever. The solution is Jesus. He is the way to a right relationship with God—the only way to holiness. And He is the way to eternal life in Heaven. Jesus is the solution we all need.

> *Even so must the Son of Man be lifted up [on the cross], that whoever believes in Him should not perish but have eternal life. For God so loved the world that He gave His only begotten Son, that whoever believes in Him should not perish [in hell] but have everlasting life. For God did not send His Son into the world to condemn the world, but that the world through Him might be saved* (John 3:14-17 AMP).

I continued to watch in silent, reverent awe. Holiness settled and stayed, creating spiritual respect and inspiring reverence. I was stupefied as I experienced quiet, unspoken waves of His presence—of His holiness—in all that surrounded me. How could anyone experiencing that ever be the same?

CHAPTER 13

THE GLORIES OF HEAVEN

The twelve gates were twelve pearls: each individual gate was of one pearl. And the street of the city was pure gold, like transparent glass.
—REVELATION 21:21

How do I find the words in an earthly language to describe the wonders of a place that exists in the eternal spiritual dimension? How do I describe a community that reflects absolute perfection? How am I supposed to tell you about things that don't exist on earth? To me, it seems a little like asking a butterfly to describe his first day of flight to a caterpillar.

Heaven is beyond earthly description. Yet, for your sake, I will try to describe it. My hope is that you grasp more about the God who loves you and the place He has prepared for those who love Him in return.

Standing with my two angel guides at the entrance of the ornate and beautiful gate that gives access to the Celestial City, I paused to glance at the angel who stood guard. *Was I allowed to enter?* I wondered. Viewing the opening, I anticipated the wonders awaiting me on the other side of the enormous wall. I had seen my name in the Book of Life and rejoiced that I was accepted as a citizen of this glorious place.

The custodian's face had the expectant, joyful look of a parent watching their child unwrap a long-desired gift. Lifting his arm, he motioned me into the gate. Without delay, I sprang forward toward the light that filled the pearlescent archway. I was about to enter the majestic Celestial City I had first seen at a distance from above when I arrived in Heaven. The breathtaking images I had viewed behind the wall were beckoning me.

Cautiously, I stepped forward into the colorful orb of light at the gate's entrance. My eagerness swelled. The brilliant light enveloped me, washing through me like a living substance. From the city center, light moved outward from its source. As the radiance traveled through the opening, it gushed like water rushing through an unexpected break in a dam. Escaping the gateway, the light spread outward into the countryside, ministering life and love to all it touched.

Heaven's light is difficult to describe because it is distinct from light on earth. The light of Heaven dances with every imaginable color—countless hues that are not visible to the natural eye on earth. The light is alive and rich with the life and love of God. It is one of the most profound things I experienced in Heaven—I don't have words to convey its magnitude.

God's life and love filled the light, strengthening me as it touched me. I felt as though I had been granted access to the womb of creation. The characteristics of the heavenly light infused me with super energy, causing me to feel as though I could accomplish anything.

Progressing through the tunnel of light, I could hear the music from the city grow in depth and increase in volume. It seemed to contain perfect love, making my spirit swell with joy.

So many have asked me questions about Heaven since I first shared my story in *Flight to Heaven*. In response, in this chapter I am attempting to address some of the most asked questions. However, be mindful that a good translation of the Bible is always the final authority. I do not recommend a modern Bible or a paraphrase. Many of these have been seriously and purposefully tainted and modified. God is still able to keep His Word undefiled, but you will need to select a solid-translation Bible, the only true authority on the subject of Heaven.

Even though I do not read others' near-death experiences, I often hear from people about differences between something I have said and what someone else's story reveals. I believe there are several reasons for this. First, Heaven is so vast and intricate, people's experiences could vary greatly, depending on what they were exposed to. However, if anyone's story—including mine—contradicts God's Word, it is not an accurate depiction.

Another reason for variations is that it is so difficult to describe a spiritual dimension in earthly language. Individuals who have had this experience may choose different words to express what they felt and saw. In addition, listeners' perception of what they read and hear can vary.

THROUGH THE GATE

The interior walls of the tunnel of light were made of the same pearlescent substance that coated the entrance. They were mesmerizing. The surfaces appeared translucent—so much so that I could not easily discern where the surface of the wall began or ended. The immense tunnel into the city was just as long as the wall was thick, making it approximately two hundred feet of glorious splendor.

Nearing the end of the tunnel that allowed me access through the wall, I gazed upon the glorious Celestial City that opened in front of me and seemed to have no end. I knew I was home. This was where I belonged. Nothing had ever felt so "right" before, and never will again until I return.

It wasn't the *things* I could see that made me feel this utter joy and sense of belonging. It was knowing I was an integral part of a precious heavenly family. I was chosen, actually ordained, to be a vital and valued member of the family of God that occupied the Celestial City.

MOST SIGNIFICANT OF ALL

One truth that is important for me to address before sharing further is that the sights I saw, the aromas I smelled, and the feelings I experienced in Heaven were the least significant things there—if anything can possibly be considered less significant than any other. Absolutely every aspect of Heaven reflects God and His love for His people. In that truth, everything has immeasurable value. On earth, people are enthralled with descriptions of Heaven they can relate to—like the sights and sounds. People more easily connect with whatever their physical senses have experienced. But in Heaven, it's the opposite—almost always.

Everything in Heaven communicates first to the spirit in fullness and revelation. Then the soul (mind, will, and emotion) interprets and understands with the intellect. The physical aspects, although significant, are less meaningful than the vast revelations of God and His love that affect all things. I bring this to your attention because when describing some of the sights and sounds, it is easy to miss the deeper eternal and spiritual aspects being conveyed.

I realize how difficult it is to comprehend the spiritual realities of Heaven if you have never experienced them personally. But I believe if you ask the Lord to enlighten your spirit to the truths of His Kingdom, He will help you know Him in all things.

May I attempt to provide you a feeble example of what I'm trying to describe? Imagine looking underwater at the colorful life forms of a coral reef—seeing plants and animals of infinite diversity, incredible detail, and amazing originality. And the colors of these astonishing creatures are indescribable.

What is the deeper truth to the beauty we see? It is this. There is a God who created all this diversity and beauty because He is the Creator. He doesn't create to impress you or me. He creates many amazing things that no man or woman will ever see. And this is the same God who created you and desires to have fellowship with you eternally.

Likewise, at every turn and with every new sight—as amazing as it all was and is—the primary thing that happened to me was gaining appreciation for the Creator and a deeper understanding of the God who loves me.

I perceived countless aspects of God every time I smelled a new fragrance or saw a new view. Each experience revealed more about His nature and His glorious, indescribable love for me and for everyone who is part of this heavenly community. How grateful I was for every new revelation.

TOWNSHIPS AND MANSIONS

My first glimpse of the townships had been from an over-the-wall perspective as I initially descended into the countryside. Now I was viewing these beautiful homes from the ground, inside the city, walking among them. Each home was unique, most of them surrounded by colorful gardens that appeared designed specifically for that living space. Collectively, a group of these dwellings formed a neighborhood community of creative perfection.

Some looked like apartments or condos decorated in flawless detail. Others were luxurious estates that reflected beauty and glory in their design. Most were more than one story high. And all were constructed with breathtaking materials—some familiar, most unfamiliar. Each home was like a work of art that continued to reflect inspired and super-intelligent design.

It was evident to me that each residence reflected the heart and soul of a Master Architect. Obviously, God had built each abode with insightful creativity, lovingly designed for an offspring He knew better than they knew themselves.

As I traveled among the townships, all the homes seemed to have occupants. However, unlike on earth, a large percentage of the residents were outside interacting with the community, as if all were closer than family. It was wonderful to see. Of course, they were indeed family. These were brothers and sisters bound together by the blood of Jesus.

GARDENS AND STREAMS

Meandering throughout the townships, I saw woodlands and parklike areas filled with fountains, streams, and gazebos where people could enjoy walking, sitting, and fellowshipping with one another. Multiple types of animals—and an abundance of colorful bird species—dotted the natural landscape and treed areas. I've had a love affair with birds ever since this experience.

It seemed that nearly every home had a porch or patio where friendly and joyful faces interacted with their neighbors. Their happy voices filled the environment as these gathered saints shared conversation and laughed—obviously enjoying one another's company.

Throughout these parklike areas, crystal clear living water flowed in beautiful fountains and natural streams, continually releasing two things: music and color. Soft melodies of glorious praise emanated from the water as it flowed and circulated. Wherever there was water, there were also gentle rainbows of incredibly brilliant color hovering over it.

The water appeared to have life within itself. When it moved, it seemed to sing and dance—all by God's design. I could easily spend more than a day attempting to describe the water in just one of the beautiful fountains. It's so alive, and its attributes are so different from water on earth.

Now this may sound strange to you, but God is present in the water. I realize that doesn't make a lot of sense from earth's perspective. But His presence is in absolutely everything because the light is in everything—the light that contains His life within it offers refreshment and life energy through the water.

All the water I saw in Heaven appeared to have life in it— God's life. It was alive but not like on earth. But alive, let's say, like a plant. But that's not exactly right either because plants die on earth. Nothing in Heaven dies. In God are life and love and light.

ANIMALS

You've probably gathered by now that life is everywhere in Heaven, and that includes animal life. There is every kind of animal in Heaven—in the meadows, forests, lawns, and atmosphere.

To me, there was something strange about the way all the animals behaved. It took me a while to recognize what was different. Not one animal had any fear. Each acted calm, natural, and unafraid. And each was highly responsive to interaction with any other life form.

Most of the creatures resembled the animals we have on earth except they were more perfect, and unlike on earth, they were able to communicate with one another and with the people. All living things in Heaven—both people and animals—know they belong to God and are an integral part of His design. As strange as it sounds, there is unity even between the animals and the people.

Just a few of the examples of the interactions I saw were people riding horses and cats and dogs playing with people in the parks and on the porches of the homes. I saw people interacting with some of the birds and wondered if all these animals were former pets from earth or different animals unique to Heaven. They were certainly regenerated to be compatible with the spiritual realm. All the animals I saw seemed to have a spiritual aspect to them.

It's sort of funny to compare the way people often handle animals on earth with the way they interact in Heaven. On earth, I frequently hear pet owners saying things like, "Get back here," or "No, no. Drop that." This would be normal communication between a master and pet here on earth. But there? It's much different. Animals and people interacted with ease and harmony—even with love.

The light and love of Heaven I speak so much about, touch and interact with the animals and the birds, as well as with the flowers and the grass. Animal life is part of Heaven's community. All the creatures behaved as if they knew they didn't have an owner like the ones on earth do. They all have the same Master—their loving Creator—just as everyone who lives in that glorious place does.

STREETS OF GOLD

The streets of Heaven were not the flat surfaces of gold I had imagined. It appeared as if they were made of translucent glass with a golden hue. There were no seams or blocks but pure, uninterrupted, transparent gold. It seemed like endless glass, so flawless that it appeared to be infinite in its depth. If I viewed the road in the distance, it did appear more like a solid surface of gold. But if I looked straight down, I could see for what seemed like forever.

The way the light moves within the depths of the roadways as it shines through, was breathtaking—another reflection of the light and love of Heaven.

THE FIRST DIMENSION

Every part of Heaven was new and unfamiliar yet seemed natural and perfect. Things were just the way they should be in the spiritual realm, or what I choose to call the *first* dimension. The spiritual realm or eternal realm is the first layer, and everything we see originates from that dimension.

On earth, that realm is invisible most of the time. Occasionally, God allows His children to gain a glimpse of the first dimension, even while we are still in our natural bodies. Although normally invisible to the natural eye, it is more real than what can be seen or felt with our senses.

Let me share just one example of something that occurs in both the natural and the spiritual realms and the differences there are based on which dimension we are in. Let's consider communication.

On earth, we think of the *heart* as the organ that pumps blood. But that's a physical part of us that dies when our body dies. In spiritual terms, "the heart" is referring to "the spirit," which is the *real* us. Our spirit is who we really are. And because our spirit is eternal, we will live forever. It is our spirit that lives in Heaven.

The *heart* is a Bible word Jesus often used to describe the spirit of a person. Jesus spoke about a man's spirit while He was on earth and said things like, *"For where your treasure is, there your heart will be also"* (Matthew 6:21). He also said we are to love the Lord with all our *heart*, soul, mind, and strength.

Along with our heart, we use our mind for communication. Our mind is not the same as our brain, which dies when our body dies.

Our mind is an intellectual part of us that is eternal and will live forever. It is the part of us that provides free will, choices, and decisions.

In Heaven, information, questions, answers, and discussion traveled directly from heart to heart, from spirit to spirit. Whether through thought, word, or deed—every being, angel, or saint—communicate from heart to heart, first and foremost. The benefit is obvious. Communication was flawless. It was complete and accurate and provided full comprehension. There were no misunderstandings. Nothing was left out. Intent was conveyed as well as emotion. And love was always the underlying force.

When I was there, I realized communication was effortless, pure, and clear. Oh, how I wish we could communicate that way here on earth. Here, it is such a struggle to try to convey a complete thought or feeling with earthly language. So much is left out, and we can be easily misunderstood.

In Heaven, there was no need to search for the right word or wonder if I had accurately understood something. Every answer I received to my questions was imparted to my heart immediately, in full, and with complete accuracy. From there, my spirit conveyed the understanding to my soul, or mind, allowing me to comprehend with my intellect.

I received both revelation knowledge and understanding of truth about whatever question or concern I had. This was not telepathy—not mind to mind. This was deeper and purer than that. It was heart to heart. No communication relied on what a person already understood intellectually. It was pure truth received and perfectly understood through revelation knowledge by the power of the Holy Spirit.

ANGELS

In Heaven, angels were as commonplace as saints. They moved about unobtrusively but with purpose. Angelic beings fulfilled many tasks, from assisting the saints of Heaven in various ways to overseeing different places or events. They were largely messengers and servants, responding to God's will.

You may wonder about the two angel guides who accompanied me from the hospital on earth to Heaven. It became apparent that they had been sent to direct my journey through the earth's atmosphere and the void that looked like deep space. They were assigned to protect me. "From what?" you may ask. That would require another book. But let me say quickly that there are demonic forces all around earth and in the heavenlies. And currently, these dark forces have a certain amount of authority and dominion. While out of my body, I needed spiritual protection as we passed through the domain of satan's forces.

While we were traveling the vast distance between earth and Heaven, I saw countless spheres of light traveling in the opposite direction—from Heaven to earth—at unimaginable speeds. Thinking back on this remarkable experience, I realize that those light spheres were God's messengers. These were angelic beings being sent from Heaven to accomplish something on or around earth—possibly in response to a prayer or to fulfill a heavenly directive from God. This makes me think of Daniel, who was sent an angel messenger from God in answer to his prayer. Yet it took twenty-one days for the angel to get through the battle of spiritual wickedness in high places that hovered over the area where Daniel was.

The two angelic guides remained with me throughout my visit, directing my journey and answering many questions, heart to heart. I saw other angels who were larger than my guides. I don't know if this is correct, but their size seemed related to the amount of authority they had. Their belts or breastplates vary in size and beauty and seemingly also reflect their heavenly assignments. I would sometimes see their intricate wings extended, but when folded, they were nearly unnoticeable.

Throughout my time in Heaven, I noticed large, beautiful gathering places where saints would congregate to praise and worship God. Angels were always joining the community in song and with various instruments. It was clear to me that angels are just as much an integral part of praising God as the saints.

HEALED AND WHOLE

You probably are already aware there is no sickness or injury in Heaven. All who enter there are whole. They are complete—spirit, soul, and body. There is perfect health and wholeness in God's presence immediately upon arrival.

No one had lingering trauma or emotional or physical pain. There was no lack of any need being met or any type of insecurity. There was no loneliness, no rejection or stress. All enjoyed living in the glorious image God planned for them from the beginning. It is such a confirmation that God's will, which reigns supreme in Heaven, includes healing and wholeness. It is no wonder that Jesus healed, delivered and met people's needs during his earthly ministry.

> *Your kingdom come. Your will be done on earth as it is in heaven* (Matthew 6:10).

UNIQUELY MADE

In Heaven, each person was wonderfully unique. And each individual quality reflected God's glory in a way worthy of joy and thanksgiving. No one felt embarrassed about anything. Not a single person was insecure. No one regretted the way God made them. Each saw the perfect plan and purpose of God in themselves and in others.

I noticed people of different races, skin tones, and features—differences that often cause distrust and division on earth. But in Heaven, the differences were never a source of division or negative distinction. Quite the opposite. God was glorified continually for the display of His perfect creativity in each person and the beauty each reflected.

The differences that divide on earth bring glory to God in Heaven and thanksgiving and praise from the people.

> *I will praise You, for I am fearfully and wonderfully made; marvelous are Your works, and that my soul knows very well* (Psalm 139:14).

UNITY

The aspect of Heaven that affected me the most was the oneness among the saints—the unity—something barely understood and seldom experienced on earth. The love bond among all the people in Heaven's community was so strong that it is not possible to fully describe. The love was incredibly evident. There was no competition. No jealousy. No malicious intent. Each citizen of Heaven exuded love and acceptance toward the others, and in that, God was continually glorified. This single aspect of Heaven ministered to me in ways that changed me and still impacts my life.

All those in Heaven knew truth and were, therefore, in perfect harmony with one another. The lack of a deceiver and of sin, allowed all to remain continually in one accord and in agreement with the Holy Spirit. Surprisingly, this mutual unity did not make everyone the same or limit individual free will. It created perfect love and joy within the community because all were beneficiaries of singular, perfect truth.

SPIRITUAL GROWTH

I was surprised to learn that not everyone in Heaven was at the same level of spiritual maturity. Some saints developed more faith and learned more about God and His Kingdom while on earth. Because of the life they lived and the spiritual choices they made, some gained deeper spiritual insight and more spiritual maturity prior to Heaven.

For example, faith grows on earth when a person resists the attack of the enemy. There is no enemy in Heaven, and resistance is not needed; therefore, faith does not grow in the same way.

As challenging as it is on earth to grow spiritually, our world provides a prime environment for many spiritual attributes to be developed amid tribulation. When dealing with fear, difficulty, persecution, and attacks, faith grows, trust is strengthened, and faithfulness develops.

I met some who had pursued God more diligently, learning His ways and allowing Him to direct their lives while still on earth. Because of earthly difficulties, some had become more purified than others whose lives had been relatively easy. It was interesting to see and recognize the differences in maturity among the saints. These differences were not a source of division but were another reason for all to praise God and glorify Him for the strength of His people.

The more mature saints were clothed in more glorious light. They were an integral part of helping strengthen and teach others what they had learned about the ways of God. There was absolutely no arrogance or pride associated with the glory that came from spiritual maturity. The interesting point for me was to learn that everyone still grows in spiritual knowledge and understanding even after arriving in Heaven.

There is no sin there. That's why there is never envy or strife or pride. There is no regret or judgment. That's why there is unity among the brothers and sisters. I'm talking extreme oneness in complete accord. There is only love and praise to the Lord for every new understanding and deeper revelation. Every testimony shares of God's goodness, deliverance, and ministry, and produces more praise and thanksgiving to the Lord.

ANSWERS TO THE HARD QUESTIONS

I previously touched on communication and how it works in Heaven, but now let me expound a bit as it relates to receiving answers to questions. Everyone has "whys" about things that happen during life. When someone enters Heaven, there are often more questions than answers, at least at first. But know this. Every question has an answer, and every question is answered when it is asked.

I think it's safe to say that everyone who arrives in Heaven comes with a desire for understanding the "why" of various experiences they had on earth. And people are continually imparted with truth about whatever they are seeking to understand. We enter Heaven with such limited perception and an earthly—even worldly—point of view. But this begins changing immediately upon arrival.

For every question, there was a righteous answer, not only an answer but also a principle based on a deep understanding of the heart of God. The answer fully embraces the question in completeness, bringing revelation and peace.

On earth, we are linear in our thinking, but in Heaven we are given multifaceted deep eons of truth regarding all our questions. Nothing in Heaven is two-dimensional. It is not about simply learning facts. It is about fully comprehending every aspect of the question and then the answer—which penetrates deep into the heart—bringing understanding, and healing, if needed.

In Heaven, we learn the heart of God regarding every situation we inquire about. And we receive as much revelation as we choose to receive, entirely in step with our questioning. In this way, we learn the ways of God and grow in harmony with each other as God's children, and with His creation.

CHILDREN IN HEAVEN

Learning is continual for all. Certainly, the small children who arrive in Heaven as aborted or miscarried babies and those who die an early death, receive instructional training. They are cared for by angels designated to impart understanding of God's plan.

Many citizens of Heaven help to instruct and love the children. These babies and young ones are taught various things—including the purpose of the cross and the gospel of salvation—a plan they did not understand prior to their arrival. As they mature in their grasp and acceptance of these truths, they are allowed to enter and participate in the general community.

Children do not remain as immature children but develop and grow in their glorified bodies as their spirit's mature. They gain spiritual maturity just as all do in Heaven, and this is reflected in the simultaneous maturing of their glorified bodies. Being an adult or a child is different than on earth. In Heaven, it's about maturing spiritually first. Then the glorified body matures in response to the spirit's growth.

Learning to conduct oneself in the fullness of the principles of God's Kingdom allows complete access to Heaven. Every new arrival goes through a certain amount of introductory training about life in Heaven before being fully incorporated into the lifestyle and community there.

EARTH IS A REFLECTION OF HEAVEN

Earth was created as a reflection of Heaven. But because of satan's deception and man's sin, earth has become corrupt and perverted. However, despite satan's best efforts, I recognize many aspects of this fallen world that remind me of the "perfect" original in Heaven—the way God intended it to be here on the earth.

Since visiting Heaven, I have heard several ask, "If God is so loving, how could He allow my child to die?" or "How could a loving God allow war and disease?"

Sadly, these questions cause me great grief because of how much *misinformation* there is in the world—misinformation about both God and the fallen spiritual world we live in here. Since my visit to Heaven, I now understand what God's desire was for humankind originally. Before the rebellion, there was such beauty and blessing. With the fall of man came the loss of the dominion God had planned for His children.

Originally, there was no disease, no war, no destruction, no perversion, no sickness, and no death. But man chose to behave contrary to God's will. Man chose to disobey and to attempt independence from God. Humankind opened the door and allowed satan to take the lead, and now we live with the fruits of satan's kingdom. This act of rebellion caused man to spiritually die, severing his connection to his Creator. And we blame God?

I'm not trying to be a theologian. I'm sharing with you intimate details about the reality I experienced in Heaven, in hope that you will learn from what I absorbed there. Please understand that the battle on earth is about good versus evil. It's about God and satan. And listen to this—it's about you understanding the truth about Jesus. Once you understand who Jesus is, what He did and why, then you'll understand God and His plan. And then everything in life will begin to make sense!

ETERNAL LIFE

God loves you and me perfectly. And He has a plan for every life. Heaven is the eternal home for those who believe and accept that Jesus is the Son of God, that He died for mankind's sin, and that He rose from the dead. Heaven is waiting for *all* who will surrender their lives to Jesus Christ and live for Him here and now.

This is the gospel message. The eternal truth that allows access to Heaven.

> *Believe on the Lord Jesus Christ, and you will be saved*
> (Acts 16:31).

It's the most wonderful and flawless plan ever. There is no downside to it. Despite mankind's sabotage of God's original plan, He made a perfect work-around to reconnect us to Himself through His only Son, Jesus Christ.

> *If you confess with your mouth the Lord Jesus and believe in your heart that God has raised Him from the dead, you will be saved* (Romans 10:9).

YOU ARE IN ETERNITY ALREADY

You are already living in eternity. Your spirit will never die. So the question is, where will you live when your body dies? With your loving Creator in Heaven? Or in hell with the angel of rebellion? It all depends on which one you serve here on earth.

We each have the right to freely choose. Even if we choose not to make a choice, we are choosing to ignore the free gift offered to us by God. As descendants of Adam and Eve, who rebelled, we are all born in sin and therefore born as citizens of satan's kingdom. We must choose to transfer our citizenship to God's Kingdom by choosing to follow and serve Jesus Christ before our body dies and we enter eternity.

> *Jesus said to him, "I am the way, the truth, and the life. No one comes to the Father except through Me"* (John 14:6).

Have you chosen?

CHAPTER 14

SEEING JESUS!

For now we see in a mirror, dimly, but then face to face.
Now I know in part, but then I shall know just as I
also am known.

—1 Corinthians 13:12

Heaven is a banquet of majesty and revelation. Being there was much like trying to drink from a fire hose—I could absorb only a fraction of what Heaven offered. Yet with every step, I gained new perspective, new understanding, and new insight.

Earthly words and language are completely inadequate to describe the richness of that glorious place, much like the futility of trying to describe a color that does not exist on earth. So why do I try? I hope your heart may grasp some part of Heaven that helps you understand the God who loves you and recognize the reality of the home He has prepared for those who love Him.

I had been traveling on the same pathway since entering the city. It was impossible not to focus on the source of the light at the city's center, the light that continued to draw me. The indescribable white light was mesmerizing and unlike any light I had experienced on earth. The light in Heaven is not limited to straight-line travel but bends and sways and curves ever so softly and gently, as if alive—and with the strength of a thousand suns.

The pathway I traveled behaved like a moving walkway—somewhat like you might find at a large airport. I'm not saying it looked like an airport walkway, but had a similar effect, in that my steps produced more travel distance than just mere earthlike steps.

Not only did I progress more than seemed physically possible, but I also felt as though my strength increased as I traveled. My journey had already taken me hundreds of miles from the gate where I had entered this glorious city, yet I was just as rejuvenated as I had been when I first arrived in Heaven's countryside.

The powerful rays of light, filled with God's life and His love, were the greatest aspects of Heaven. This could be why my energy did not dissipate. The light beams were continually arching from the center of the city outward—touching, infusing, and ministering to everything and everyone—including me.

From within the beams of light, the triune God imparts Himself to all of Heaven. For me, the fact that these heavenly rays contain three aspects—light, life, and love—is a testimony of the Trinity. God the Father. God the Son. And God the Holy Spirit.

FATHER, SON, AND HOLY SPIRIT—THE TRINITY

The concept of the Trinity had always been somewhat of an enigma to me. I'd heard people try to explain it using an illustration of water. Water can be found in three forms—liquid, gas, and solid—and yet it is one substance. Nevertheless, I still had difficulty grasping the essence of a triune God, and the water example didn't change that. How could God be one yet have three forms? It had never made much sense to me, until I visited Heaven.

My perspective instantly altered once I arrived in my eternal home. The Trinity was absolute. Three-in-One was now obvious. Genius, in fact.

Heaven operated perfectly because of the Trinity. Now I understand part of what Jesus said in Scripture, *"on earth as it is in Heaven."* The Trinity is the foundation of how God has chosen to operate in Heaven, as well as on earth. I learned more about God by understanding more fully about the three aspects of the Trinity as they are in Heaven.

God is a Spirit. God the Father, is the Head and center of all. He rules Heaven. His word is the structure and His will is in harmony with His word on everything. His word and His will are as one. He governs every realm in existence.

Jesus is the Son of God. He is God given to man. He and the Father are as one. Jesus lives in a glorified body in the form of man so God can interact and express Himself to man in a way that can be comprehended. Jesus is God *with* man. Even His name *Immanuel* means "God with us."

Jesus is man's way to God. No one can enter God's presence without the right standing or righteousness that Jesus offers. Jesus is also the active and creative Word of God. He takes God's will and puts it into action through faith to bring about the manifestation.

Then there is the Holy Spirit, who hovers like a gentle mist—barely perceptible—permeating all of Heaven, watching, listening, touching, managing Heaven's affairs perfectly. He sees all things and keeps all of Heaven in agreement with God. The Holy Spirit continually ministers to each one who is part of Heaven's community.

The value and role of the Holy Spirit cannot be overstated. Everywhere throughout Heaven, the attributes of the Holy Spirit are present. I quickly learned to love the Holy Spirit and understand Him to be a person. Before visiting Heaven, I had never acknowledged Him—most likely because I had received almost no teaching about Him.

The Bible says the attributes of the Holy Spirit are love, joy, peace, patience, kindness, goodness, faithfulness, gentleness, and self-control. I experienced these perfect expressions of godliness while in Heaven. They allow for complete unity and love to reign unhindered.

While in Heaven, it was easy to see how the Holy Spirit is a precious companion and guide to all of God's children. He is the Comforter, Teacher, and Gift-giver. Eventually, I discovered that each new insight I received, each piece of knowledge I gained, and every revelation that was given, came from the Holy Spirit. He is ever present, and He continually enhances, strengthens, and ministers to all the citizens of Heaven—personally and perfectly.

Heaven is a spiritual realm. It's a real place that exists in the first dimension. In Heaven, I discovered that truth was always revealed directly to my spirit first. There was never confusion, nothing left out. Each message was complete and came with full understanding—spiritually, intellectually, and emotionally. After a revelation of truth was presented to me, my spirit would share the new understanding with my mind. Once in my mind, this fresh understanding became knowledge.

What I just tried to describe may sound vague or ambiguous, but please try to comprehend it because I believe, by God's design, both Heaven and earth operate this way. I think the Bible agrees with this in principle.

I realize how backward this process is on earth. It's no wonder that there are so many different interpretations of what is true. In Heaven, everyone knows the truth. All are in complete unity, because truth is disclosed through the revelation of the Holy Spirit.

> *"For My thoughts are not your thoughts, nor are your ways My ways," says the Lord. "For as the Heavens are higher than the earth, so are My ways higher than your ways, and My thoughts than your thoughts"* (Isaiah 55:8-9).

HOW CAN ANYONE UNDERSTAND GOD?

Only a regenerated spirit empowered by the Holy Spirit can grasp the eternal truths of God. We are not able to worship Him with our mind alone. We must worship God with our spirit and in truth. There is freedom in truth.

The Holy Spirit is an integral part of Heaven. He is the conduit of communication between God and man. And He is the source of truth and unity throughout Heaven. Likewise, the Holy Spirit is the source of truth and authentic unity on earth.

Later, back on earth, I discovered a passage of Scripture that describes an event in which each part of the Trinity operated on earth within their particular roles, all at the same time. Read below and see if you agree.

> *Then Jesus came from Galilee to John at the Jordan to be baptized by him. And John tried to prevent Him, saying, "I need to be baptized by You, and are You coming to me?" But Jesus answered and said to him, "Permit it to be so now, for thus it is fitting for us to*

fulfill all righteousness." Then he allowed Him. When He had been baptized, Jesus came up immediately from the water; and behold, the heavens were opened to Him, and He saw the Spirit of God descending like a dove and alighting upon Him. And suddenly a voice came from heaven, saying, "This is My beloved Son, in whom I am well pleased" (Matthew 3:13-17).

In this passage, God's voice was heard by those present at the baptism. The Bible says the voice came from Heaven. At the same time, the Holy Spirit came out of Heaven to earth in the form of a dove. The Holy Spirit confirmed that Jesus had been sent by God, and the Holy Spirit equipped Jesus with the power of Heaven for His earthly ministry.

There it is—Father, Son, and Holy Spirit. All Three in one place at one time, each being a distinct aspect of God in order to fulfill God's plan and purpose. This scriptural illustration of the Trinity in action, I carry with me every day.

MUSIC

Intensely noticeable to me were the faint, melodious harmonics that make up the music that fills Heaven—soft melodies and harmonies in minute detail that blend perfectly and are utterly wonderful. I was greatly impacted by Heaven's music. From the time I arrived, music filled me. Praise continually reverberated through my entire being, inviting me to add my thanksgiving to the chorus of worship that filled all of Heaven.

It may sound strange, but even the flowers and trees give praise to God in music. In our eternal home, absolutely everything—plant, animal, water, saint, and angel—continually worshipped God in one way or another.

The atmosphere of Heaven is alive and powerful. I'm referring to the *spiritual* atmosphere. There was not a moment of time, or anyplace in all of Heaven, where the atmosphere was not filled with the music I keep trying to describe. I just can't seem to find adequate words to express the melodies of praise I can never forget. And the Holy Spirit's presence was always in the music.

This was not just any music, but the most precious, wonderful, and inspiring melodies of joyful praise. Many songs and choruses were sung at the same time but without competition. They blended to form a more perfect song. And the sounds of voices and instruments drifted throughout Heaven, resonating with incredible and beautiful tonal precision and richness. The music of Heaven was glorious and continually ministered to me in profound ways.

I'm not a music expert in any way, but the organization of the different sounds and frequencies to make music incredibly pleasant, arranged, composed, and interesting to my spirit, ministering to me at my deepest levels. The musical notes had frequencies that I don't believe exist on earth. Or if they exist, we can't hear them. Today, I believe music is designed by God and exists primarily in the spiritual dimension. Heaven sensitized me to music and the frequencies it contains.

THE CITY CENTER

Finally arriving closer to the center of the city, I could see the concentration of light in front of and above me. Ahead, a massive stairway had come into view. Although it was still in the distance, I could see it perfectly, as if it were close enough to touch.

My visual sense, like my other senses, was enhanced and perfected. Nothing ever looked faded or blurry. Whatever I focused on was immediately visible in perfect detail, from the nearest flower to the farthest mountain top. It was the same way with the staircase I was approaching.

I quickened my pace and arrived at the bottom step, eager to ascend. The light was more brilliant at the stairway—more than anywhere else I had yet seen. Light behaved so differently in Heaven, almost as if it had weight and substance. It drifted down the stairs from above, making me think of the way smoke flows.

Every color imaginable was in the light. It started as the purest of white but also looked to me as though it had been fractured by a prism. I could identify seven distinct colors—but that was just the start. These seven colors were altered into additional shades and hues, creating an infinite number of colors. I have not seen anything close to it before or since.

This colorful light hovered on the staircase, moving slowly and gracefully downward until it surrounded the bottom of the stairs and diffused into the lush gardens. It was the most colorful and elegant visual display of light I had yet witnessed, and reassured me I was getting closer to the source. With every step I took, my anticipation grew. I wondered, *Will I see Jesus?*

The wide and regal staircase was the most beautiful I had ever imagined. Its width was at least half the length of a football field. And each step was deep, allowing plenty of room for many to stand and fellowship wherever they chose. The stairs were made of white marble with veins of gold threaded through them. The stairway curved gently as it ascended until it disappeared into the light above.

A golden railing of intricate design bordered each side of the stairway. Living, flowering vines wove their way through the rails, wrapping and embracing the golden lattice.

On earth at age nineteen, when all this took place, I had never been one to pay much attention to things like flowers or intricate details of creation. I was more of a "machine" kind of guy and loved working on anything mechanical. My comfort zone had always included things that were logical and physical. But Heaven changed me. There, I was in awe of the intricacies and the perfection in all God's creation. Every detail captured my attention and revealed more of God to my spirit. For example, the soft fragrance of the flowers that accessorized the stairway mesmerized me and filled me with joy.

THE STAIRWAY

For a moment, I stopped to soak in the beauty of the stairway and the activity on it. Dozens of angels and saints were traversing up and down the steps in both directions. Some stopped to interact with others as they passed. At the same time, from my perspective, all of them seemed to have a distinct purpose in their planned destination.

It was obvious that people had plans and missions in Heaven! There were things to do and tasks to complete. Each effort strengthened the community and further enhanced what was already perfect. Angels also had assignments to serve God and man. They faithfully fulfilled their purpose both in Heaven and on earth.

No one was in a hurry. And even though hundreds were moving up and down the stairway simultaneously, it did not look crowded. There was harmony in everyone's movements, and perfect unity did exist—indescribable unity!

This is the part I noticed first and loved the most. Unity. Being in one accord. It was glorious.

A large angel was positioned at the bottom of the stairway. Dressed somewhat like the angel who had greeted me at the gate's entrance, he looked magnificent. This angel no doubt possessed great authority. As our eyes met, he smiled in recognition. I could tell he was expecting me.

Inside my heart, I had a natural, compulsive desire to ascend the stairway toward the source of the brilliant, pure, white light. No one told me who or what was up the stairs. But again, there was a "knowing." Somehow I knew it would be the throne of God. Jesus would reside there also.

I understood that God was the source of the light that filled Heaven and that the light contained within it love and life. I knew the origin of the light was up the magnificent stairway.

Imagining that Jesus would be there gave me a profound desire to ascend, but I also realized approval from the angel was needed to advance. Once again, communication was exchanged heart to heart. In this way, the transference of thoughts and ideas remained pure. Nothing was misunderstood. Nothing needed was left out. That was part of the reason it was so concerning when I received the angel's message. "No, Dale. You are not allowed to go up."

What? Pardon me? Really? Then I spoke, "May I ask why not?" I felt compelled to ascend the stairway. I *needed* to go up. Everything had been drawing me to the origin of the light since I had arrived in Heaven.

The angel responded lovingly and patiently, "You can't go up and still go back."

My mind began racing. *Go back? Go back? What are you talking about?* Everything I had ever known—family, friends, school, flying—had been of no importance to me since I had arrived in Heaven. I hadn't thought even once about my life back on earth. All I wanted or needed was here in this glorious place.

Earth life is just a testing ground. It's preparation for Heaven. Sadly, most on earth never understand this and get this fact thought backwards. I sure did before my heavenly journey. My earth life was like the front porch of a glorious house full of bright light, music and wonderful people who loved me. Once inside, I never gave the front porch another thought.

At the stairway, I understood. My entire existence was for one purpose: to have eternal life with God in Heaven. Plus, the most wonderful family to be a part of was here. My heavenly family! I belonged *here*. Life in Heaven was the only thing that mattered to me.

But with the angel's words came a fleeting memory of my earthly life rushing back into my mind. I had no desire for it. This new perfect life was where I belonged now. I was made for Heaven. Heaven was made for me. I did not ever want to leave this place.

THE LAMB OF GOD

Then the angel moved one large step to the side, revealing the One behind him. Before me stood the most regal and beautiful man I had ever seen or could imagine. His piercing eyes penetrated my heart. They were filled with wisdom, gentleness, and kindness. *Agape* love exuded from those deep eyes of pure goodness. There are no eyes on earth like them. In His eyes were total authority and total acceptance.

He was the source of the light I had been searching for. He smiled as He greeted me, His face radiating living light.

Gradually, I became aware that this was not the first time we'd met. I knew Him. He knew me. I knew some things about Him. He knew everything about me. He knew even the deepest parts of me! This was Jesus—my Savior and Friend! This was the Lamb of God. Jesus! Jesus my Lord!

My knees buckled. I couldn't stand. My legs lost their strength, and I collapsed. Both my hands embraced His feet. I remained motionless on my face before Him, holding His feet.

Such majesty. Such authority. Such holiness. The power. The love.

Just then, I felt unworthy. I was experiencing inner conflict as I became aware of my personal inadequacy to be in such a glorious, sinless place with the Son of God. *Of course, I'm unworthy. Look at this place. I'm nobody, a nobody of the tallest order.*

He knew my thoughts. At the same instance that I felt unworthy, I was filled with images of His sacrifice. I saw how His blood had covered and washed me clean. My sin had been pardoned by Jesus. Jesus, the Messiah, had given me right standing with God.

In the fifth grade, when I was eleven, I had heard the gospel of Jesus. The Bible taught that He sacrificed His life for my sin. That was when I had repented and been forgiven of my sins and turned the control of my life over to Jesus. That was when Jesus Christ had become my Savior and Lord.

I *was* worthy to stand boldly and without shame—because of Jesus. Apart from believing and repenting, my worthiness wasn't because of anything I had done. It was because I had accepted what Jesus had done for me. As part of the family of God, I had become an heir of salvation and inherited the benefits He provides—which include eternal life in Heaven.

The assurance that I belonged there was clear. It was all because of the One standing before me. His presence was like air. Jesus was my *everything* in that moment. Fifty years later, He is still my everything.

Both my hands continued to hold Jesus's feet. I stared, surprised to see the damage from the nails. There were no scars, only holes in His feet with brilliant light emanating from them.

One thought coursed through my mind over and over: *How could You love me this much? Why would You love me this much?* My second thought was, *I owe You everything!*

In a somewhat feeble way, I worshipped the Lord. Not raising my head, I clung to His feet, not wanting to let go.

He leaned down close to my bowed head and spoke, "Do you love me, Dale?"

I tried to speak but couldn't open my mouth. I was overwhelmed. I wanted to speak out of my mouth what my heart believed, *Oh, yes! Yes, I love You, Lord. I know who You are and what You did for me. You gave me life. I'm sorry I've been so selfish and such a disappointment.* But instead, I didn't utter a syllable. For that moment, my mouth ceased to work, but my heart ached with worship.

Then He bent down further, moving closer to my ear. I can still feel and smell His sweet breath on my face. In a reverberating voice, He whispered, "What will you do with the life I give you?"

Saint Joseph's Hospital—Burbank, California

In my first waking memory, I found myself lying in a hospital bed as the sound of glorious music faded away.

The old me was dead. That old Dale Black, the highly driven, self-centered, arrogant young athlete and pilot, was dead.

Now I could truly live.

CHAPTER 15

WALK BY FAITH, NOT BY SIGHT

The lamp of the body is the eye. If therefore your eye is good, your whole body will be full of light. But if your eye is bad, your whole body will be full of darkness. If therefore the light that is in you is darkness, how great is that darkness!

—MATTHEW 6:22-23

Following the airplane crash, while hovering over my broken form in the operating room and separated from my physical body, I had little concern for the massive injuries I had sustained. But later, every bit of the damage from the crash would affect my life in very personal ways.

One of the serious injuries received in the airplane crash was a gash that cut deeply across my forehead, down through my right eyebrow and my right eye. The iris, cornea, pupil, and what is called the posterior chamber had been sliced by crash debris.

The emergency room medical team did their best to keep the damaged eye stitched and in the socket. It was only much later I learned that no one expected me to see from that eye again.

Soon after the crash, a specialist was summoned to operate on my seriously damaged eye. Following that surgery, my eye was bandaged and a black patch placed over it. At that point, there was nothing more to be done but wait and pray.

The many challenges I faced were punctuated by occasional victories. Those moments were always an emotional and spiritual oasis in a vast desert of need. Much sooner than anticipated, I was released from the hospital and heading home. Everyone knew my early release was miraculous. Although I was confined to a wheelchair, it was thrilling to see the sky and smell fresh air again. Children still looked at me as if I were a monster, but I was happy to be alive and continually thanked God for a second chance.

With only one arm working, one eye to see from, my broken back in a brace, and my left leg and ankle in a full cast, I couldn't do anything on my own. However, I struggled to achieve any independence I could.

Every time a bandage was removed or a cast came off, I regained another piece of freedom and was encouraged in my journey of faith.

Dr. Graham had been slow to share the full details of my injuries with me. He later explained that, because of the extensiveness of the damage, he had thought it best to reveal the specifics only as it became necessary.

Over time, I learned I'd broken almost every bone in my body. Since I was entirely preoccupied with more noticeable injuries, I didn't ask many questions about the extent of the damage to my eye. Then during one of my routine doctor visits, I was surprised to learn that I was fortunate to still have my natural eye at all. And if I was lucky, I might eventually see light and dark, but would never be able to read with it. For someone still dreaming of flying professionally someday, that was about the worst news I could receive.

Abundantly obvious to everyone except me was the realization I would never live a normal life. And, of course, I would never fly as a professional pilot. But I was in serious denial of those facts and unwilling to accept that reality.

It was the late 1960s. Unlike today, it was an extremely competitive time in the field of aviation. The average "new hire" pilots had a BA degree, all the required aviation licenses and ratings, as well as 3,000 to 5,000 hours of flight experience already recorded in their logbooks. And still, there were twenty qualified applicants for every airline job opening. Not only was 20/20 vision a requirement, one had to possess natural and uncorrected vision in both eyes.

With my eye so severely damaged, the prospect of ever being accepted as a professional pilot was relegated to the faith department, much as the healing of all my other injuries were. The amount of damage was overwhelming, and the battle was definitely uphill.

I engaged faith in a determined quest to regain my vision— both spiritually with prayer and through exercise, putting my faith into action.

A verse I found in the Bible gave me hope and strengthened my faith. Second Corinthians 5:7 says, *"For we walk by faith, not by sight."* When I read those words for the first time, I knew God was talking to me. If I wanted to see again, and fly again, then I needed to do so *by faith*.

There was more. This Scripture convicted me to use faith not only for my eye, but also to live my entire life by faith. I knew God was asking me to walk through life by faith, not by sight. That revelation formed the way I have lived my life ever since.

Even though my body and memory had sustained massive injuries, my spiritual life was vibrant. I turned to God for every challenge—and there were many. Changes that were brought about by feeding on God's Word daily, reflected in my new, developing faith.

The only part of me that was apparently not damaged was my heart. In fact, it was somehow flourishing flourishing in the midst of the mess I was in. Since the moment I woke up in the hospital, my heart was working the way hearts are supposed to work.

Throughout the healing process, I experienced great trust and understanding of God and His promises. Learning about the way God heals became a primary focus of my bold faith.

During this time, I began wondering how I could research subjects in the Bible and find answers to my questions. I had so many questions that needed answers. That's when I learned about the concordance in the back of my Bible. I learned that is where I could find Scriptures that contain the word or subject I was interested in. This new resource provided a never-ending treasure trove of discovery.

An exciting new world opened to me through my Bible. Next, I discovered an even better Bible study tool—an exhaustive Bible concordance. With an old King James Bible and my Bible concordance, I started a lifetime journey of learning more about God and His ways. It was like discovering the combination to a safe filled with treasure.

I continually prayed and thanked God for healing my damaged eye so I could see once again. The problem with my eye had launched my exploration of His Word. As I looked up Scriptures about the "eye" in the Bible, I was astonished that God had much to say on the subject.

In Matthew 6:22-23 (KJV), Jesus stated, "*The light of the body is the eye: if therefore thine eye be single, thy whole body shall be full of light. But if thine eye be evil, thy whole body shall be full of darkness. If therefore the light that is in thee be darkness, how great is that darkness!*"

At first, I didn't understand what this Scripture meant. But as I continued to dig, even at the age of nineteen, alone and without anyone else to discuss it with, I learned from God's Word. Although we have physical eyes to see *natural* things, we also have spiritual eyes to see *spiritual* things. That's what Jesus was describing. If I wanted to find answers, I needed to make sure my body was full of spiritual light.

During the struggle to regain my sight, I also stumbled on the greatest discovery of life. I found out I could ask God a question and He would answer! The Bible taught me that I wasn't bothering God to ask Him questions. In fact, He wanted me to pursue Him.

Learning to listen to God, proved to be the greatest discovery of all. Before, I had always spent more time *talking* to Him and almost no time *listening*. This single revelation about listening for God's response changed everything.

I asked Him questions about what Jesus meant in those Scriptures about the eye. Then I listened. "*The light of the body is the eye.*" Jesus was saying that the light of a person's soul (the mind, will, and emotions) is controlled by that person's spirit. The Scripture continues, "*if therefore thine eye be single*"; I learned that the spirit of man should have one purpose, a single focus—to glorify God.

Next, Jesus said if you have the single purpose of glorifying God, "thy whole body shall be full of light. But if thine eye be evil, thy whole body shall be full of darkness." As I continued reading, verse 24 stopped me in my tracks: *"No man can serve two masters: for either he will hate the one, and love the other; or else he will hold to the one, and despise the other. Ye cannot serve God and mammon"* (Matthew 6:24 KJV).

Researching this in the original language, I discovered that *mammon* doesn't represent only the love of money. Money certainly was not what I was after. I needed to *see* again. I learned that *mammon* means "wealth regarded as a false object of worship and devotion." It means anything of this fallen world that is placed in a position higher than God. Anything.

This passage of Scripture was describing to me that spiritual commitment and maturity—where the heart is focused—reveal whether our eyes are full of light.

Being confined to a wheelchair was the perfect place for me as I began this journey of faith. I couldn't work or get distracted with much. I was stuck and had one thing to do: learn about God and work with Him to heal my body.

These Scriptures in Matthew were teaching me how to develop into a mature follower of God—a disciple of Jesus. They were also somehow guiding me to think about my eye as being controlled like a muscle. Choosing to move and focus my spiritual eye on godly things helped me translate those principles into my choice to move my physical eye and focus it on particular objects by my will.

I did a little research and found that the eye requires muscular dexterity to focus. I reasoned, without asking anybody, that I should exercise my eye muscle if I wanted my natural sight to be strong—just as I was learning to discipline my spiritual eyes to be spiritually strong.

I was already working out my right arm and my right leg (the only limbs not in a cast at this point). Since they were getting stronger with exercise, then why not do the same with my right eye? The process seemed logical and followed godly principles.

Carefully removing the patch covering my injured eye, I placed it over my good eye. At that point, I couldn't see anything. Even though I felt foolish, I looked toward the window and recognized that it seemed slightly lighter than the area around it. Making every effort to focus my damaged eye, I kept trying to see something—anything—until my eye hurt too much to continue.

Every day I followed my new regimen, trying to get my right eye to focus on something. During this time, I discovered a small book about having better vision through exercise, and began following the suggested procedure. It seemed futile since nothing was even visible, not yet anyway. I was committed to continuing in faith. It was equally important for me to speak aloud Scripture promises about healing—proclaiming their authority over my body and situation. I knew my faith was growing stronger because I was reading God's Word aloud according to Romans 10:17 (KJV): *"So then faith cometh by hearing and hearing by the word of God."*

Just as my natural eyes were created to see natural things, my spiritual eyes could discern spiritual things. Likewise, my natural ears could hear natural sounds, but my spiritual ears could hear God's Word and turn that truth into faith.

Learning to access God's promises using the Word of God was more exciting than I can explain. God's Word was, and still is, so alive, and through faith, able to accomplish anything God desires.

In John 15:7, another truth exposed itself and landed deep in my heart: "*If you abide in Me, and My words abide in you, you will ask what you desire, and it shall be done for you.*"

I was inspired when I found this Scripture because I was asking God for something I desired. Since the word *abide* was the condition to receive the promise, I looked the word up and found out it means "to remain stable or fixed in a state."

That meant if I remained constant in my relationship with the Lord, seeking His will and giving Him first place, then I was abiding in Him. And if I remained close to the Lord and His Word, then my desires would align with His desire for me. From that position, I could ask with confidence for something He already wanted for me, and according to His Word, I would receive it.

The more I read the Bible, the more my faith grew. The word *faith* is such a key word throughout Scripture that I looked that up, too, and found myself reading Hebrews 11:1: "*Now faith is the substance of things hoped for, the evidence of things not seen.*"

Reading the footnotes in my Bible, the original Greek word for *substance* also means "realization," and the word *evidence* is like "confidence." I reread the Scripture with those additional meanings, and it read like this: Now faith is the substance and realization of things hoped for, the evidence and confidence of things not seen. The word *realization* means it's real to me. *Substance* indicates weight and form—something real. Faith reflects that I believe something in my heart so strongly that it is as if it's already mine. In fact, it is so real to me that it *is* already mine. And confidence in the reality of what I'm believing for brings it into my possession as evidence of my faith.

In addition, the first word of the verse is *now.* That got my attention, too. As I thought about why that word was there, I realized that faith is always in the now. It's never in the past or the future. It's right *now*—in the moment. In the present is the only place faith can live. These new revelations were changing my entire understanding of how God works and how we are to conduct ourselves on earth in agreement with how it is in Heaven.

I felt as though I was on a treasure hunt—God was leading me from truth to truth, teaching me His ways. His ways are opposite of the world's ways. And I realized that, for the most part, His ways are not the ways of the modern Church. From my observation, the Church is more like the world than the Kingdom of God. What I was learning was transforming.

The world says, "I'll believe it when I see it!" But God was telling me that faith is believing *before* I see it!

Every day, I continued to exercise my injured eye. Covering my good eye, I repeated the exercises until the muscles ached with fatigue.

I would cling to Scriptures I found in the Bible. Scriptures like Mark 11:22-23: *"So Jesus answered and said to them, 'Have faith in God. For assuredly, I say to you, whoever says to this mountain, "Be removed and be cast into the sea," and does not doubt in his heart, but believes that those things he says will be done, he will have whatever he says.'"*

This Scripture taught me about the power of the spoken word. Jesus had spoken the world into existence (see Psalm 33:9).

And I was created in His image. In the passage in Mark, He was telling me to speak to the obstacle and command it to be removed and then not to doubt. I was learning to walk, not only by faith, but also in the ways of God and His Kingdom.

Mark 11:24 taught me more about how faith works. *"Therefore I say to you, whatever things you ask when you pray, believe that you receive them, and you will have them."* It was important for me to learn the order of faith.

I was told to first ask in prayer. Second, to believe—and keep believing. Third, after asking and believing, then I would receive. Receiving was the final step in this process and would come only when I was finished with the believing part. That meant I had to believe until I received, however long that took. The entire world began looking different as I grew in my understanding of these principles of faith. I truly felt I was bringing Heaven to earth as I learned what God's Word said and then took action in agreement with that.

I had to make a decision every time I read or spoke God's words. Do I really believe God's Word is true? Or are these Scriptures just inspirational words that comfort me and make me feel better? Jesus spoke the words I was reading for a reason. They are specific. Again and again, I chose to believe they were true for me in my situation.

Day in and day out, I continued. Whenever I spoke about my eye or exercised it, I spoke aloud the promises of God, one after the other, over and over. Like a dog with a bone, I would not let God's Word depart from my mouth In other words, it was constantly in my mouth and I spoke about it at every opportunity.

God taught me so much as I put His Word into action for the two years following the airplane crash. I barely recognized myself. I knew God. I understood His ways. I had truly learned to walk by faith. His Word had been proven true in my life again and again

God's Word is impeccably accurate and entirely true. And He is faithful. Most believers know He is the God of the supernatural, but many fail to understand that He is *also* the God of the natural realm. If He created both the natural (physical) and supernatural (spiritual) realms, then why would He not use both realms to answer prayer? The answer is simple: He would, and He does!

God created the natural and supernatural realms and works in and through both of them simultaneously.

As I had turned to the Lord for the healing of my injured eye, He responded to my faith in both the spiritual and natural realms. He answered my prayers through the actions I took in faith, and in response to my words. For example, exercising my eye took place in the natural realm while at the same time I was praying and claiming His Word for healing in the spiritual realm. The two together gave me the results I was asking and believing for.

This combination of both realms has worked again and again during the fifty-plus years since this truth was revealed to me.

Taking action is a vital part of receiving answered prayer. God teaches us that *"faith without works is dead"* faith (James 2:26). God and I were in a partnership. Together, we stood in faith in His promises. Together, we took action as an extension and reflection of faith. Together, we saw answers to prayers of faith in action.

As Christians, we cannot simply know something to be true and expect to receive the associated promise. Knowing is different from believing. If a person knows about the four forces that are in effect for an airplane to fly, that's good. But that doesn't mean he's a qualified pilot or can successfully fly an aircraft.

If we want to receive the manifestation of God's promises, we must *believe* in agreement with that knowledge and *take action* as an extension of our faith to *receive*. We must act upon what we know to be true. Our action Our action reflects our faith through our commitment to to the outcome we are believing for.

God faithfully honored His word to me, as always. Consider my injured right eye, which I had been told might see light and dark—if I was lucky. In two short years, my vision improved gradually through faith until I was able to pass the FAA First Class Flight Physical vision test with 20/20 uncorrected vision. Although the manifestation had seemed gradual, looking back, it had been dramatic and miraculous.

I never wore glasses or contacts or underwent any type of vision-enhancing surgery. My vision was restored through walking by faith. I applied both the natural and supernatural realms to receive the answers to my prayers.

God is faithful and always leads us to the truth we need. Our job is to diligently search for it until we find it and then to walk in in agreement, using spoken words and actions.

For an entire forty-year career in aviation, I continued to use the eye exercises and to speak God's promises aloud—faith in action.

Every FAA Flight Physical I passed was a first-class exam. And each test resulted in 20/20 uncorrected vision.

Praise the Lord! He is good and faithful to perform His Word.

In this chapter, I described much about our physical eyes. They are indeed important. But even more important are our spiritual eyes. Jesus said, *"But blessed are your eyes for they see, and your ears for they hear"* (Matthew 13:16).

Always keep your focus on the Lord and His ways. As you grow in your relationship with Him and in His Word, your spiritual vision will grow more than you can imagine possible. That's what happened to me—and it can happen to you.

If you would like to understand more about the eye exercises I used to strengthen my vision, I have included a description and diagram in Appendix A near the end of the book.

CHAPTER 16

DYING TO SELF

Then Jesus said to His disciples, "If anyone desires to come after Me, let him deny himself, and take up his cross, and follow Me."
—MATTHEW 16:24

nvisible injuries are often the most difficult to deal with. Upon waking up from the three-day coma, I quickly realized my memory was a disaster—most of it was missing.

Despite the void of my past, new revelations became evident and proved far more important than my history. For starters, I understood that the Bible contained supernatural information about God and how He works. I knew I could trust Him completely. I realized God's Word is the structure that holds all things in place. God and His Word had become my new foundation for living. How did I know these things? I still wasn't sure, yet I knew it was somehow connected to the airplane crash. And I knew with all my heart that the words in the Bible came from God.

Following the crash, my life largely revolved around my extensive injuries. My body had suffered physical trauma that had produced a long list of damage. Both legs, both ankles, both arms, and my back were broken. My left side had absorbed much of the impact of either the monument or the ground, causing tremendous injury to my left shoulder and my left ankle; in fact, according to my doctor, both had been "destroyed." In addition, I had sustained multiple lacerations from aircraft debris, with my head and face taking the most serious damage.

In addition to what doctors called irreparable damage to my sight, my face sustained multiple lacerations; one particularly deep gash had nearly removed my chin. My nose had been broken and flattened. My entire body had been soaked in aviation fuel, triggering much of my skin to peel off in thick layers. And my head had been shaved to remove pieces of shrapnel and allow countless stitches to close the many lacerations on my scalp. I was convinced I looked like Frankenstein—a fact often confirmed by those who saw me.

Over time, through thirteen surgeries and other treatments, much of my body was healing. And I was grateful to be out of the hospital. However, as a young man with my future still ahead, it was my left ankle that concerned me most. Although I had been in a leg and ankle cast, using crutches for close to a year, the ankle was still not healing. I was surprised. I had seen so much of my body recover quickly in what others proclaimed were miracles, but my ankle wasn't getting any better. *Will I have to remain in a cast forever?* I wondered.

Dr. Graham was known as the doctor of the stars, having performed surgeries on more movie actors and sports celebrities than anyone in the country. His number one patient, who couldn't perform without him, was daredevil Evel Knievel. I knew God had arranged for me to have the best surgeon possible, as Dr. Graham had been on call at St. Joseph's Hospital the morning of the airplane crash. I trusted him and thanked God that Dr. Graham was my primary doctor. But that was not enough to prepare me for the news that was coming. Dr. Graham hadn't spoken much about my ankle during other visits—there had always been so many other issues to focus on. But during this doctor's visit, he had difficult news for me regarding my left ankle.

"Your ankle isn't healing, Dale. Can you see that?" We both looked at the x-rays up on the screen. "The blood has quit circulating through the bone. The bone is dying. It's called avascular necrosis, and it's serious. If you ever want to put weight on your left leg, we need to do another surgery and fuse bone from your hip into your ankle. With this type of surgery, you'll lose all mobility, but you'll probably be able to put weight on it. You'll be able to walk with only a slight limp."

I was trying to absorb the information but could hear only one thing: I would never play football or baseball, run, or fly again. I could feel my heart thumping in my chest—faster and harder. *That can't be God's will for me!* Panic began setting in.

Dr. Graham stressed, "You need bone fusion surgery before the bone is completely dead! We don't have much time, Dale."

"What if I don't do the surgery? What would happen?" I held my breath, hoping for an answer I could live with.

A frown formed on the doctor's face. "That's not a good option," he responded. "The bone would die. The ankle would become brittle and eventually collapse. At that point, there would be nothing we could do to fix it. You'd be a cripple."

My thoughts were spinning. I needed to figure things out. At that moment, all I wanted was to leave Dr. Graham's office as fast as possible. Grabbing my crutches, I headed for the door, dismissing the doctor by mumbling, "I'll pray about it, Doc. I'll get back to you when I hear from God."

The last words I heard as the door was closing behind me were, "This can't wait, Dale. I'm trying to help you. Let me know...soon!"

What kind of answer is this? I tried to make sense of what I had just heard. I had read the Scriptures about Jesus being my Healer. Isaiah 53:5 says, *"By His stripes* [I am] *healed."* The Lord had healed everything else I had prayed for. *Why not my ankle?* I had a serious decision to make. And right then, I needed answers, so I headed toward my grandpa's office in Long Beach, California.

Looking at him from across his desk, I shared what the doctor had told me. I spilled out my questions, concerns, and fears. Barely giving him time to grasp my challenge, I leaned forward. "What should I do, Gramps?"

"Dale, the Bible says in Hebrews 11 that faith is the substance of things hoped for, the evidence of things not seen. That means that what you see, feel, or hear isn't the final word. Don't be moved by your physical senses or the circumstances of your situation. I'm not telling you to ignore what the doctors say, but above all else, believe what God has said. Do what God's Word and your heart are telling you to do."

He went on, "God cannot fail. And it is impossible for God to lie. Dale, your faith must be in God and in His Word." Grandpa looked into my eyes to see if I understood what he had told me.

Then he continued, "First of all, pray. Pray by yourself, and then pray with others who have faith in God and His Word according to James 5:14. Just make sure that those you are praying with really believe God *will* answer your prayer."

I pulled out some paper and started writing a checklist. "Okay, Gramps. *Pray.* Got it. I should pray and then ask someone I trust—someone who has faith—to pray with me." I decided right then that these instructions would become my Answer to Prayer checklist.

Grandpa continued, "Okay, Dale. Second, read your Bible."

"Read where?"

"God will show you. Just start reading." Grandpa elaborated, "Something in the Bible will jump out at you and speak directly to your heart. God's Spirit will lead you to find what you need. Just ask Him to lead you…and then expect to find it. Don't stop looking until you do."

Being young and spiritually underdeveloped, I thought all this sounded pretty strange, but I committed to do everything on my new checklist. I trusted my grandpa. Therefore, I trusted what he was telling me.

Grandpa hesitated, waiting for me to finish writing. Then he continued, "Third, Dale, do exactly what God reveals to you, but be prepared for your faith to be tested. In my experience, God will always allow a test to strengthen your faith. Understand, it is not God testing your faith, but He allows the enemy to test it to determine whether you really believe in your heart what He has promised. And remember this, Dale: God's will is what you're looking for. And His will is found in His Word. He'll never violate His Word. Once He reveals His will to you, you must come into agreement with it and stay in agreement."

Grandpa's words burned into my heart. I was sure I would never forget a single thing he had told me. Nevertheless, I carefully folded my checklist, tucking it securely into my shirt pocket. I was determined to follow every step to the letter.

Now that I had shared my fears and hopes about my ankle with Grandpa, and he had given me a plan to follow, I needed to talk to him about something else—an equally difficult subject. I shifted in my chair, trying to find a comfortable position as I adjusted my cast and braces. Grandpa leaned forward and peered intensely into my face. "What else is troubling you, Dale?"

Grandpa and I had always been close, but since the airplane crash, we had spent a lot more time together. I knew he loved me. He communicated his love by always taking time to listen when I needed it—which was often these days. And he was a man of faith whom I trusted to give me solid spiritual advice.

Better known as Russell Price, my grandpa commanded a great deal of respect among his peers. Everyone who knew him thought of him as a man of principle who possessed an iron backbone. And he was known as a man of his word. The most important things in his life were God, family, church, and his business—in that order.

Of course, I loved and respected Grandpa. That's why I went to his office that late afternoon. After gathering my thoughts, I told him about my returning memories of the crash. Next, I nervously confessed that I had observed my unconscious body on the operating table at the hospital.

Cautiously, I began to share a few of my vivid memories of Heaven, wanting to "test the waters" and see if he'd believe me or think I was crazy. I briefly described the massive wall, the people I had met, and the glorious music. Then I paused, and Grandpa spoke up.

"Dale, before you continue, may I say a few things?"

"Sure, that's exactly why I'm here," I responded.

"During my lifetime, Dale, I've observed many people who have used supernatural experiences to gain accolades from others. A lot of books have been written about this, and some of these people go around the country speaking on the subject to fan the flame of self-promotion or to see financial gain. Not all, of course, but it's an easy trap to fall into. And I do not believe that pleases the Lord.

"Dale, when you're dealing with things like Heaven and eternity, you're operating in God's realm—the spiritual domain—and I think you need to be cautious. If God has truly allowed you to experience these things, they're sacred, aren't they?"

I looked into his wise and loving face but didn't say a word.

"Dale," he continued, "I don't question for a second that the experiences you remember are real. I've known you all your life. And I know your heart. If God has given you a glimpse of Heaven, in my opinion, you have a couple of options. You can speak about what you saw and heard, *or* you can let your life be a reflection of your sacred experience. By that I mean, live out whatever you believe you saw. Live out what you heard and what you learned. Your life's actions will speak more strongly than your voice. Above all, let the Lord lead you, Dale. Follow the Lord."

Moments passed without a word being spoken as he gave me time to process what he'd said.

Finally, my grandpa muttered these words while staring out his office window: "That might explain why you had no internal injuries or major brain damage." Wiping tears from his eyes, he whispered, "Well, praise the Lord."

I thanked him for taking the time to talk with me and hobbled out of his office.

As I drove toward home, I began to pray, "Lord, You created everything that exists." I paused, subconsciously holding my breath. It was as if God had just shown me how the power of His spoken Word, coupled with His faith, created all things in existence. So much suddenly made sense.

"Oh, God, You are so completely awesome! You made my ankle. You know exactly what's wrong with it and how to fix it. Father, I've read in the Bible that Jesus healed everyone who genuinely asked. He didn't turn anyone down. And the Bible also indicates that healing is available to everyone. So I believe it's Your will to heal me, too. I completely believe in my heart that You want to heal me and restore my ankle."

Arriving home, I decided to hop into the house on my strong right leg. The skin under my arms was overdue for a break from the constant rubbing and pressure of my crutches. Without a moment's hesitation, I made my way to my bedroom and picked up my Bible. I held it in my hands for a few minutes, wondering where to turn and what to read.

I prayed, "God, You have something special to say to me through Your Word, right? Please tell me where to read."

I waited for a moment. Then the number *seven*, followed by *Matthew, chapter seven*, entered my mind as if it were a photograph. At first, I assumed this was just my imagination, but the mental picture did not fade. "Okay. Matthew, chapter seven," I mumbled.

Somewhat skeptically, I turned the pages until I found the seventh chapter of Matthew. *"Judge not, that you be not judged. For with what judgment you judge, you will be judged"* (Matthew 7:1-2).

What does this have to do with my ankle? Maybe I misunderstood how this works. Verse by verse, I kept reading. And then it happened, just as Grandpa had said it would. My eyes fixed on verses seven and eight, and they leapt out at me as if they had my name printed all over them. The words seemed to grab me by the neck and shake me. My heart burned as I read:

> *Ask, and it will be given to you; seek, and you will find; knock, and it will be opened to you. For everyone who asks receives, and he who seeks finds, and to him who knocks it will be opened* (Matthew 7:7-8).

God had led me to this simple yet profound statement of faith, words that had challenged His people for centuries. I prayed, "God, You said that everyone who asks, receives, and he who seeks, finds. That means me! Right now, I ask You to heal my ankle so I can walk and run someday. Thank You, Father. I believe You are answering this prayer even now."

In that very moment, the decision was made in my heart. "Lord, I'm making a choice. I'm deciding to believe You are answering my prayer to heal my ankle. I am asking in faith that You do what is impossible in the natural because Your Word says all things are possible with God.

"God, if I'm ever going to walk again, if I'm ever going to play sports again—" Tears ran down my face as my prayer continued, "God, if I'm ever going to fly again, it will be because You have healed me according to Your Word. I trust You, Lord, and I believe Your Word is true! And I will give You all the glory."

Standing up, I boldly declared, "God, I believe that it is not Your will for me to have this bone fusion operation! I respect Dr. Graham, but You will be the One to perform this operation in Your way. And I believe someday I will have normal use of the ankle You gave me.

"Thank You, Father. Thank You," I whispered, wiping the streaming tears from my eyes. It was settled in my heart. From that moment on, the course was set, and the flight plan had been filed. Under His wings, I would be carried to the destination of His choosing.

LIVING LIFE AS A REFLECTION

Over the next few days, another decision was settled in my heart. I committed to live out what I had learned in Heaven. I decided not to share my sacred experiences with anyone until God clearly told me otherwise. And I knew Grandpa would keep my secret. So I asked God for the strength to live a life that would reflect all He had shown and taught me.

The next day, I phoned Grandpa. He was pleased to hear my decisions but reminded me, "Don't take your eyes off God's Word, Dale. His promises don't change just because circumstances do." I thanked him for his counsel, thinking I understood exactly what he meant with his words of caution.

Then I phoned Dr. Graham. I wasn't braced sufficiently for his very different response.

"Dale, you're making a *serious* mistake! You're gambling with your ability to *ever* walk again." I could tell by his reaction that I would not receive any support from him for my decision. "We have a tiny window left to do this surgery. Once the ankle bone is dead, fusion is not possible. Like I told you, if you don't have the surgery, your ankle bone will collapse, and there will be nothing we can do. You'll be unable to walk on it. Arthritis will set in, and you'll be in severe pain for the rest of your life. Dale, there's no cure when that happens. Are you understanding me? You're a smart young man. Do you realize how serious this is?"

Dr. Graham's words were difficult to hear. His tone was even harder to bear. He genuinely cared about me and my future. I told him how much I respected him and how much I appreciated all he had done for me, but that this was something I had to do. "Doc, this is my decision. I've made it, and it's final, sir! God will heal me."

I believed God was going to let me fly again. And if I was ever to do that, I knew it would not happen with a fused ankle. A pilot cannot work the rudder or the brakes with a fused ankle, let alone find an airline that would hire him. I had made my decision in faith, but I'm sure Dr. Graham thought I had made it in foolish arrogance. Regardless, I was the one who would live with the consequences of my choice.

Determined to follow Grandpa's checklist to the letter, I dialed the Ferguson's number.

"Hello, Mrs. Ferguson? This is Dale Black. I wanted to ask you and Howard to pray about something for me." Howard was an elder in our church and a man I knew I could trust. They were also close family friends who knew all about the airplane crash and had been praying for me ever since.

Without hesitation, she responded, "Of course, we will, Dale. What is it?"

Quickly recounting the first item on Grandpa's checklist, I shared what was needed. "In James chapter 5, the Bible says that if anyone is sick to ask the elders of the church to pray. I'm asking God to heal my ankle. It had started healing, but then the healing stopped. I don't understand it, but now I believe God is allowing my faith to be tested. He is going to restore my ankle 100 percent. But I need some believers to pray in agreement with me. Would you and Howard pray for God to restore the blood circulation in my left ankle?"

Excited to have this step taken care of, I went outside to catch some fresh air and think about my next task. My neighbor, young Terry Smith, was outside in the yard and asked, "How are you getting along, Dale?" Terry's father was a retired airline pilot I had spoken to many times about my dream of following in his footsteps.

Terry's question provided me with an opportunity to speak about my faith in God's Word regarding my ankle, and I took it. "Well, Terry, I'm getting along great! God is completely healing my ankle, and I'm very grateful. How's it going with you?"

Within two hours of reading the seventh chapter of Matthew, I had decided not to have the operation to fuse bone from my hip into my ankle. Other people were now praying in faith for my ankle to be restored. And now I had spoken words from my own mouth about my belief in what God had already done in response to my prayer.

Soon, I realized that the first person who needed to be entirely convinced that God's Word was true was the person in the mirror—me. I didn't understand it all at first, but as I repeated promises from the Bible and spoke aloud about them to others and myself, something wonderful was happening inside my heart. Those Bible promises were taking root, and I could tell my faith was growing stronger.

"Now faith is the substance of things hoped for," I reminded myself, *"the evidence of things not seen."*

There was a kind of exhilaration to this new experiment in obeying God's Word. Because of my inexperience, I was not prepared for the pushback the enemy had in store—discouraging words, disappointing circumstances, and devastating medical reports.

To start with, almost everyone in my life thought I was making a huge mistake. One of the most difficult warnings came from my father when he heard I had decided not to have the bone fusion surgery recommended by Dr. Graham. He strongly weighed in on the situation. "Dale, you're being unrealistic and making a big mistake."

It was difficult to disagree with my dad. He was a strong individual—the president of his own successful company. He had also seen me through the aftermath of the crash without a complaint. But now, Dr. Graham and the specialists were urgently suggesting an operation that I was rejecting, and Dad didn't understand why. Nevertheless, I stood my newfound ground. "I've made up my mind, Dad. I've asked God to heal my ankle completely, and I believe He is doing exactly that."

When I returned to the college campus, I had dozens of opportunities to express my faith that God was healing my ankle. Although I was on crutches, with my left leg and ankle in a cast and my left arm barely working, every time a friend asked how I was doing gave me an opportunity to respond in faith. "God has healed me. Praise the Lord! As soon as I have new x-rays taken at my next doctor's appointment, I'll prove it! You watch. You wait. You'll see."

When my next doctor's appointment came around, eight friends—eager to see a miracle—accompanied me. We crowded into a friend's old green Cadillac and headed for Burbank. As we drove, I reminded them of our purpose: "You guys are going to be eyewitnesses to an awesome miracle."

We cruised along excitedly, parked, and descended on the doctor's office like a troop of zealous soldiers. Upon entering, I figured I'd take one more opportunity to make a declaration of faith—this time to Dr. Graham. As the nine of us walked into the exam room together, I confidently explained to the doctor, "They're here to see proof that God has healed my ankle."

The x-rays were taken. We waited in anticipation. A few minutes later, Dr. Graham came back into the room with the x-rays in hand.

"Wait, Doc. Before you show us the x-rays, we'd like to pray and thank God for the miracle." Dr. Graham stopped and respectfully crossed his hands, still holding the x-rays. He waited as we thanked the Lord for healing my ankle. After we said amen, Dr. Graham placed the negatives on the screen to begin his analysis. We all gathered around, waiting to hear the good news.

He paused for several anxious moments before speaking. Then he broke the news. "There is absolutely no progress. I'm sorry, Dale. Blood is not circulating in your ankle."

The war I was fighting was far from over, and that unexpected news showed me how ill-equipped I was for spiritual battle. I was vulnerable and untrained—and only starting to understand how important it was to put on the armor of God. I was at the beginning of spiritual boot camp and had no idea what was waiting for me.

No one knew quite what to say. My group of friends were stunned. "Don't worry, Dale. God's not finished yet!" Dave tried to encourage me as we walked toward the car. The others offered their own cautious sympathies. Looking back, I realize that none of us understood what had just happened or why.

Telling my friends that I'd rather not talk, I stared out the Cadillac's side window, deep in thought. No one knew what to say to me anyway. I needed some answers from God—and I needed them now! *Don't give me all those neat little clichés. It's my life, not Yours. I'm the one who can't walk.*

My shock had quickly turned into anger. I thought about the cold facts. *God did not do what He promised me He would do. God let me down. He blew it, and I don't like it at all! I've acted like a fool by trusting Him.* My mind considered the possibility that Dr. Graham was right. Maybe I had made a choice that would leave me more crippled than I dared believe. *If that's true, then what am I going to do now?*

Suddenly, I remembered the checklist! And the test. *Is this what was happening? Is God allowing my faith to be tested?* I recalled Grandpa warning me that once I took action with a stand of faith, my faith would be tested. I had already told a countless number of people that my ankle was healed. But what had I done when the x-rays came back with a negative report? I had believed the report more than God's Word! I had failed the test.

Feeling ashamed and frustrated with myself, I got back into God's Word and continued to plant it in my heart. Gradually, my faith overcame the fear and doubt.

Within days, I was giving my testimony again at the college chapel service. I shared my renewed faith in God and His Word as I explained what I had learned about the importance of patience and long-suffering when standing in faith. Following my update, Chaplain Welsh anointed me with oil and led many in prayer for the bones in my ankle to be healed.

With my faith rebuilt, two weeks later I invited any who were interested to go with me to Dr. Graham's office for another opportunity to see a miracle. "My faith was tested," I explained. "Now we'll see the miracle God promised." Just as before, the well-worn green Cadillac made its way toward the doctor's office in Burbank, filled with friends anxious to see a miracle.

Thinking that I finally understood what had happened, I was confident that the keys of faith and healing were in place in my mind and heart. Little did I know that the most important lessons about God and His will were just ahead of me. What I was about to learn would not only shock me but also transform me forever.

Now faith is the substance of things hoped for, the evidence of things not seen (Hebrews 11:1).

CHAPTER 17

LOSING LIFE TO FIND IT

For whoever desires to save his life will lose it, but whoever loses his life for My sake will find it.
— MATTHEW 16:25

B ack in Dr. Graham's office, the x-rays were taken. Five of my college friends and I gathered around the viewing screen again. I explained to the doctor briefly what had gone wrong the previous time. I told him how I had failed to realize my faith must be rooted in the promises of God and not in circumstances. I had forgotten that my faith would be tested before I received God's promise, but now I was ready. My friends and I held hands and prayed, thanking God for His love, for His faithfulness, and for His Word.

Dr. Graham placed the negatives on the screen. On this occasion, it took the long-suffering doctor even more time to speak.

Finally, he turned toward me and reluctantly revealed his findings. "Dale, I'm sorry." He was clearly stressed and trying to manage his frustration. "Not only is there no progress, but we have waited too long. There is no blood circulation in your ankle at all. There is nothing we can do to reverse the situation now."

He pointed at the x-ray. "That bone is completely dead!" Turning, he walked out of the room without another word.

What? I was stunned. *How could this be?* I had done everything on my checklist. I had corrected my error. This was not the way things were supposed to work. My thoughts and questions could not be contained. As far as I was concerned, the news was as bad as it could be, and I was devastated. If I could not trust God, then I could never trust anyone or anything. Ever.

As my friends and I made our way back toward campus, no one said a word during an excruciating hour of intense silence. To make matters worse, my ankle bone burned with pain inside the cast, as if reminding me of the mistake I had made.

No one was more relieved than I when we arrived back at the dorm. Without a word, I grabbed my crutches and hurried as fast as they could carry me to my room. Once inside, I slammed and locked the door. The overwhelming doubts and fears that crowded in felt as if they would crush me.

You're a fool, Dale Black. You're a stupid fool to go against medical advice and to put your complete trust in God. Everyone else was right, and you were wrong! You obviously don't know what you're doing, and now you'll never walk again. You can forget about sports. Flying is out of the question, forever. All because of your idiotic faith experiment. God doesn't heal everybody. It was a big mistake not to have that bone fusion operation, at least you could have walked again. But no, you had to act like some big man of faith. Now look at what you have. Nothing. Welcome to the world of lifetime cripples. How could you be so stupid, Dale? Now you've lost everything.

Because of my many injuries and broken back, it was extremely difficult for me to sit comfortably. The most pain-free position was on my knees leaning over the edge of my bed, and that's exactly where I found myself. Broken. Desperate. Angry.

There wasn't a person on earth I wanted to talk to. Only God. But what I had to say to Him was not particularly reverent. "God, You've blown it! I've made an absolute fool of myself in front of the medical staff and my friends. Not only that, but we've made a real mess of making my life into anything that gives You glory. Worst of all—for me anyway—my vocational goals have come to a dead end. And now I'm crippled for life, with severe arthritis just around the corner. How can this be Your will for me?"

I was way out of line, and I knew it. Still, I continued my selfish rant, "Why didn't You do what You said You would do in Your promises in the Bible? Is this some kind of cruel joke? I did everything on the checklist. I did all of it, but You didn't keep Your part of the deal. What else do You want from me? Do You really want me in a wheelchair for life? Is that it? Well, that's exactly what You've got!"

I felt completely lost, angry, and alone—as though I had been abandoned in the middle of battle. In the silence that followed my self-centered temper tantrum, I heard a clear yet gentle voice in my heart, "Dale, why do you want to be healed so badly? Seek first the Kingdom of God, and His righteousness, and all these things will be added to you."

I had read that Scripture recently—several times—but somehow I had just passed by the part about seeking His righteousness. Tears began to stream down my face, and once more I sensed Him speaking, "Seek Me first. And My righteousness, Dale. And all these things will be added to you."

I knew exactly what He was telling me. I should have been seeking the Healer more than the healing. I had wanted a miracle more than I wanted the Miracle Worker. His words continued to resound in my heart, "*My* righteousness."

Despite my outspoken faith and Christian talk—despite all my immense effort—I knew there were still hidden sins I hadn't dealt with. My stubborn demands for healing were right at the top of the list. Sure, I believed the answer to my prayers would glorify God, but I was really more interested in what *I* would get out of it.

Amid this convicting interaction with the Holy Spirit, my heart shifted. I gave Him *everything*. I finally allowed Him into every part of my life. I gave Him full and complete control. "Lord, I'm so sorry! I know that every day I live is a gift from You. It's so obvious to everyone, especially me, that I should have died in that plane crash. I choose to trust and serve You, whether I'm in a wheelchair or not. Again, dear Jesus, I am so very sorry."

I've seen Heaven—how can I still be so self-centered? I couldn't understand it. How had I gotten so far off track? I fell before the Lord and wept.

I wept as if my tears could wash away the adventurous life I had dreamed of for so long. Words poured out of my heart to the Lord, "I give up my obsession to walk again. I give up flying, sports, my quest for respect from others, everything, Lord Jesus. My future is in Your hands. I will continue to pray for healing because I believe that is Your will for me according to Your Word. But this time, You are in first place, first place in my life now and forever. I want to fulfill *Your* dreams for me—not mine."

Right then I decided that, no matter the cost, I was going to serve Him with my all heart. I gave up my selfish goals and plans.

I really did! "God, if You can use me better as a twenty-year-old in a wheelchair, as a cripple, then not my will, but Yours be done." I didn't just say the words. I meant them with my whole heart.

At that moment, something happened to me that I had not heard about before. I experienced a physical sensation that felt as if a heavy, rich, oil-like substance were being poured over my head, then flowed down, covering every part of me. The feeling was overwhelming. It is something I will never forget. As this was happening, joy and peace filled my heart to overflowing. For the first time since waking from the coma, I felt completely free!

A few days later, I was asked if I wanted to share an update at the Wednesday night chapel service, as I had done so often during the previous weeks. Instead of talking about my faith for healing, I shared a very simple message about surrender, about submitting to God in every area of life. I didn't mention my ankle this time. My communication with everyone switched from talk of a miracle on my ankle to having a broken will and submitted heart toward Jesus.

When it came time for my next appointment with Dr. Graham, I didn't invite others to come—I went alone.

It had been two weeks since I had surrendered my entire life to God—fourteen days since I had felt the warm "oil" flow over me and since I had resigned myself to life in a wheelchair if God could use me better that way.

Driving toward Dr. Graham's office, I found myself deviating a little off course. A few moments later, I arrived at the familiar Valhalla Memorial Cemetery, where I pulled over and stopped just a few feet from where our airplane had crashed at the Portal of the Folded Wings. On numerous occasions, I had come to this spot where it seemed natural for me to connect with God. Maybe it's because this was the place where I had left my body. Or maybe it was because this was the spot where I had learned I was already living in eternity. It was also the place my friend and flight instructor had died. Whatever the reason, this was where I often came to ask God questions and listen for His answers.

Sitting on the grass next to the huge mausoleum, I reviewed in my mind the sequence of the aircraft smashing into the monument, my body falling to the ground, and then the "real me" hovering above. There, at the monument, I again marveled at the miracle of how God had spared my life.

On this day, my mind reviewed the checklist—the one I had followed during the previous months. Only this time, I renewed my love for God and vowed once again to serve Him for the remainder of my days, at all cost.

Getting back in my car, I drove through traffic along the familiar streets to Dr. Graham's office, only a few blocks away. Unlike previous visits, I quietly entered the waiting area alone and smiled at the familiar face of the receptionist. Then I whispered a prayer, "I am Yours, God." There were no expectations. Nothing was held back. There was only a desire to be the person God wanted me to be.

Dr. Graham greeted me. He was more reserved than usual and seemed surprised that I was alone. He updated me on all my injuries before taking routine x-rays of my ankle. After a short wait, he placed the images on the viewing screen. I didn't bother to look this time. I noticed that Dr. Graham stared, pondered, but didn't say a word. He glanced at me with a brief look of confusion.

Then in a gentle voice, he whispered, "Your ankle is healing, Dale." He looked back at the images, shaking his head. He continued to point at the screen.

My eyes fixed on the x-rays, trying to understand what the doctor was saying.

"The blood in your ankle has started circulating again. I don't understand it, and I cannot tell you why. But Dale, your ankle has healed more in the last two weeks than it has in the last six months combined." He lifted his eyes and looked into my face as if he might find the answer there. He shook his head one last time. "I don't understand this at all."

In the sacredness of that moment, deep within my spirit, there was a resounding echo, *"He who loses his life for My sake will find it."*

CHAPTER 18

HEAVEN TO EARTH

"For My thoughts are not your thoughts, nor are your ways My ways," says the Lord. "For as the heavens are higher than the earth, so are My ways higher than your ways, and My thoughts than your thoughts."
—Isaiah 55:8-9

At the beginning of this book, I shared with you what happened in the cockpit of a Boeing 727 on approach into LAX. Remember the voice? "Dale, this is your last flight…for TWA."

For me, there could be no doubt who had spoken. It was the voice of God. He has spoken to my heart in this same way many times since waking from a coma after the crash. But that night in the cockpit, God's "voice" was referencing a career-changing situation.

You would think that having experienced this prompting many times, coupled with my trust in God, I would not have struggled with His words. Yet I did. Truthfully, I did not want to give up my career for TWA. *Was God really asking me to give up flying forever?* At the time, I didn't know.

Isn't that so often what we do? When God tells us something we would rather not hear, we try to dismiss it. Maybe, we decide, it's just our imagination. Or we think the enemy is trying to trick us. Well, I had those same thoughts as I fought for my desires for several hours. I sat in the back of the airplane as the ground crew began preparing for the next morning's flight.

For me to resign from TWA was a lot to consider. I had paid dearly for this career—years of focused effort and a lot of hard-earned money, which came out of my own pocket. Flying was the adventuresome life I had dreamed about since my early teens. Giving up this job would be permanent. There would be no coming back or going to another airline once I left, if I left, not with my medical background. I had already exhausted every other airline—almost 200 of them—prior to applying at TWA. And my injuries were always the reason I was not hired. It had been a miracle that TWA said yes. I knew God had opened that door. *So why would He close it now?*

From my wife's perspective, resigning would be asking her to give up a successful lifestyle, lucrative pension and retirement package, insurance, and unlimited free travel benefits—all the things she had expected to have as security and benefits to enjoy throughout our lifetime. She, too, had worked hard to help me get into the cockpit of a US air carrier.

But of course, there was the other side. I was a living "dead man," and I knew it. I should have died as the others did in the crash. But God had miraculously spared my life. And then He showed me Heaven, and taught me about faith and His ways. He performed miracles on my body and restored me to health. In reality, I *had* died in the crash. Everything I had—every breath—God had given me. Who was I to make any demands on God? Sure, I told Him my thoughts, my desires. But at the end of the day, the only thing that mattered was obedience to His leading.

It would take years to fully understand what actually happened the night I heard the voice in the cockpit of the Boeing 727 at 34,000 feet. But, yes, that *was* my last flight. Not my last flight as a pilot—not by any means. But it *was* my last flight with TWA.

Was it truly God's voice? You be the judge as you read a *sampling* of how God used me once I surrendered my dreams—for God's plans.

Ultimately, I flew another thirty years, logging thousands of hours in the most incredible airplanes and flying into the most amazing places on earth. God led me to do many things that seem impossible to man, yet with God nothing is impossible. God took what I gave Him—my dreams of adventure and flying for a major US airline—and He gave me priceless, life-changing, eternally significant experiences in return.

Of course, the Lord directed me on some of the most adventuresome and breathtaking flights imaginable. Always for His purpose and glory. There were too many experiences in aviation to even begin to tell you. Such as flying a jet in perfect weather at 500 feet for hundreds of miles above nothing but the white glaciers of Greenland. Flights to resort islands in the Caribbean and off the coast of Mexico. Destinations where large airline carriers can't land, and flights most pilots would never dream of being able to fly.

While logging thousands of additional flight hours in numerous types of corporate jets and multi-engine airplanes, I've been honored to lead teams of lay ministers all over the world. We accomplished the most important work on earth—eternal work—as God led us through the most breathtaking adventures of faith.

Over and over, I have seen God do what is impossible with man. And He has accomplished the miraculous using regular people who had faith to believe. He still heals, delivers, and saves where there is faith to believe. There are too many true stories to recount. Someday, I'd love to tell you about them all.

Through the Jet Charter and Jet Sales company my wife Paula and I started and expanded, we had access to the many aircraft we managed, and we used them to fly missionary journeys around the world. God led me to train and transport lay ministry teams for the purpose of preaching the gospel, providing food and clothing, distributing gospel tracts, providing medical and dental help, and showing the *Jesus* film to countless thousands in well over 50 countries. Lives were changed as God's will was brought from Heaven to earth. Here's a small sampling of the adventures of faith.

GUATEMALA

Following the 7.5 massive earthquake in Guatemala in 1976, I landed the first plane to touch down following the quake. Our MU-2 was brimming with medical missionaries and supplies. Within days I returned with another load of medical supplies and ministry teams in our Citation II.

Out of that Guatemalan experience, came the building of an orphanage for very needy children—many of whom came out of the earthquake with injuries and trauma. This gave hundreds of damaged and orphaned children protection and care as well as the opportunity to learn about Jesus, God, and the Bible.

ISRAEL

Another of thousands of flights, involved leading a group of prayer warriors to intercede for the nation of Israel. God asked me to organize a series of flights in a Cessna Caravan over the entire border of Israel, praying for the nation's protection. Flying over every mile of Israel's border required special clearance, which we received from the government.

Additionally, our team was invited to an extraordinary meeting with the prime minister and given special seating in the Knesset. Looking back, we saw God's divine purpose for these prayers of intercession, as this occurred just prior to the scud missile attacks against Israel in 1991. We did not the future, but God did, and He looked for someone responsive to His leading whom He could use.

MEXICO

One late afternoon, as our team was returning from a missionary trip where we saw the lives of hundreds changed, I landed our plane at a small airstrip in southern Mexico for fuel. We had the thrill of walking into a group of nearby shanty homes and praying for a man who had never walked in his life. Our evangelistic team preached about the healing power in Jesus's name. Not only was he miraculously healed, to walk for the first time, but his entire family and many of his neighbors believed in Jesus after seeing God move so supernaturally. They showered us with gifts, and we had great favor to distribute Bibles and preach the gospel to many. Many received a taste of Heaven on earth.

There are not adequate words to describe the joy of being in the center of God's will. In the next three chapters, you will read examples of how God works when we exchange our ways for His.

Now it's time to begin again. I know I keep saying that, but it seems to be the way God works—new beginnings, a new life of bringing Heaven to earth. I know that visiting Heaven changed me on the inside, changed me in ways I am still figuring out.

Before the crash, I had been a driven young man determined to reach my goals of success. But after experiencing Heaven and learning who God really is, I was transformed. The fire that had driven me for selfish things, now drove me to pursue the things of God—eternal things.

An umbilical cord had been cut. My love for the things in this world grew so pale in comparison to the reality of Heaven. Daily, I find the need and desire to again die to self, pick up my cross and follow Him.

If I had to summarize *some* of what I brought back to earth from my experience in Heaven, it would be the realization that Heaven is more real than earth. Hell is just as real. Many question that, if God is loving, how could there be a hell? But God is holy, and He is also just.

I learned that the Bible is a spiritually alive, supernatural book. The words within are living and trustworthy. They will never fail. His Word has infinite integrity and is the structure that holds this world together. When God says something— anything—that settles it. That's what you will see in the following testimonies and stories where God led me through His Spirit's voice and His Word.

Heaven taught me that there are no limits with God. If I let go of my wants and desires, and allow God to lead, I can experience the life without limits He had planned for me all along.

These stories that I will share with you in the following chapters are not my stories alone. No, they are adventures of faith in God working in my life and the lives of those involved. As you read, ask yourself, "What could happen if I chose to listen to God's voice? What could happen if I were to obey that voice?"

Well, you be the judge. Are these adventures in faith because God had a divine plan for my life? Or are these adventures available to anyone who chooses to step out in faith?

There are no fewer than a hundred more stories of God bringing Heaven to earth that I could share with you. Possibly the Lord will have me write another book to reveal a few more. But for now, here are several. I hope you'll be blessed.

CHAPTER 19

LOST IN THE GRAND CANYON

What man of you, having a hundred sheep, if he loses one of them, does not leave the ninety-nine in the wilderness, and go after the one which is lost until he finds it?

—Luke 15:4 NKJV

It was Easter Sunday. My wife, Paula, and I arrived at Uncle Jack's house in Long Beach for Sunday dinner with our large extended family. Before praying for the meal, Jack asked us to remember Don Johnson and his family. Don, a member of the local church our family had attended for generations, was missing—lost in the Grand Canyon.

Don had been part of a church group that had hiked into the canyon and back up to the rim on the same day. Realizing he'd left his jacket on the trail, Don said to the others, "Go on ahead. I'll catch up." Now, five days later, he still had not returned and searchers had not found him.

Paula and I knew Don and his wife, Virginia, but we weren't close. Yet as we sat down to eat the Easter feast before us, neither of us could take a bite.

My stomach churned. As illogical as that reaction was, I had learned years earlier to recognize the still small voice of God. The Holy Spirit was definitely speaking to me. I looked at Paula and whispered, "Can you believe Don is still missing?"

My heart was pounding, but my logical mind interrupted. *This isn't my responsibility. I barely know Don. We don't even attend that church anymore. And it's Sunday. Tomorrow, I have huge responsibilities in our jet business.*

Flight students from several countries had already flown in for a jet-type rating class with my company. I was scheduled to lead the class and conduct pilot training in the morning. How could I possibly leave? Our company had tens of thousands of dollars at stake.

I'm being unrealistic to even consider jumping into the middle of this situation. It has nothing to do with me.

A spiritual and logical tug-of-war was raging inside me. Since the turmoil within both of us was preventing us from enjoying the meal, Paula and I went to the backyard to talk. Before I could catch myself, I blurted out, "I think God is asking us to get involved in this. Not sure why, but it feels like the Holy Spirit is saying we have to do something. What do you think?"

I was surprised when Paula so quickly agreed. "I'm feeling that too, and I think you're right. I don't know what, but we're supposed to do something."

Before experiencing my visit to Heaven years before, I had not been tuned in to the Holy Spirit or His way of communicating. But since returning from my heavenly visit, I am always listening—listening with spiritual ears and discerning with a sensitized heart. When I sense God's gentle prompting, I am never tempted to challenge it. Instead, I pray for understanding, listen for verification, then obey.

Later in life, I learned much from God's revelation to Elijah:

> *Then He said, "Go out, and stand on the mountain before the Lord." And behold, the Lord passed by, and a great and strong wind tore into the mountains and broke the rocks in pieces before the Lord, but the Lord was not in the wind; and after the wind an earthquake, but the Lord was not in the earthquake; and after the earthquake a fire, but the Lord was not in the fire; and after the fire a still small voice* (1 Kings 19:11-12).

God speaks in a still small voice, and I had learned to hear it. At Jack's house on Resurrection Sunday, I had no doubt God was speaking to me. And He knew I would obey.

It started with a thought: *How can I sit here eating this wonderful meal when Don has been alone, freezing, and without food for five days?* Then a Scripture hit my spirit with great clarity. I shared it with Paula:

> *What man of you, having a hundred sheep, if he loses one of them, does not leave the ninety-nine in the wilderness, and go after the one which is lost until he finds it? And when he has found it, he lays it on his shoulders, rejoicing.*

And when he comes home, he calls together his friends and neighbors, saying to them, "Rejoice with me, for I have found my sheep which was lost!" (Luke 15:4-6).

"Oh, Dale! I was thinking that same Scripture! We have to search until he is found. God has a plan to find Don!"

I nodded in agreement. "We're not going to search for a body. We're going to find Don and bring him home alive. Just like the lost sheep! Search until he is found!"

It was clear. The Lord was confirming what He wanted us to do. Paula would stay home to handle the pilots, using our other instructors for the time being. She'd run the company as best she could and help me with whatever was needed. I would begin a search for Don.

"I'll get my car and drive out there to assess what's happening. The Lord will let us know what to do. Why don't you call Virginia and find out if she wants to go with me?"

We excused ourselves from the family luncheon. Time was of the essence. I grabbed Paula's hands. "Let's pray right now that He'll guide us and bring Don home like that lost sheep." I prayed, "God, please give us whatever we need to accomplish Your will. We will obey Your leading, and we'll search until Don is found!"

Within two hours of hearing about the unfolding drama in the Grand Canyon, I was driving toward the canyon with Virginia. All the way there, I focused on building her faith in God's promises. "Virginia, when God says something, He does it. We've got to believe that. We must stay in agreement with God no matter what circumstances we encounter. Can you do that?"

"I'll try," she said through tears. "I'm just so afraid. It's already been five days."

Statistically, Don had almost no chance. An average of 250 people go missing each year in the Grand Canyon. About 29 of those die from hypothermia. After four days, the chance of rescue drops dramatically to 9 percent. After five days, the statistics drop to less than 1 percent. We would arrive at the scene on day six. The stats were strongly against us, but God had spoken. I internalized the still small voice. *Search until he is found!* We had to keep our faith intact.

We arrived at the Canyon Hotel late at night. Early the next morning, I connected with the Arizona Search and Rescue (SAR) team to ask about their progress. The team leader, Steven, was an ex-military Army Reservist about my age. His team was mostly ex-military people, plus some civilian volunteers. When I said I was there to help, his face clouded. I introduced Steven to Virginia. He made it clear he didn't want anybody influencing his search plans and protocol. He told us the best way to help was to leave him alone to do the mission he had been assigned.

About two hundred people had been searching on foot the first day. That number had now dropped to seventy. The SAR team had one helicopter searching from above. And after five full days of looking, there was still no trace of Don.

Chuck, from the church group, had refused to leave. He filled me in. "Don was wearing tennis shoes, jeans, and a long-sleeved shirt. No hat or gloves. And we don't know if he ever found the lightweight jacket he lost."

Even this late in the season, cold, unforgiving snow covered the ground—in places up to four feet deep. I could only imagine what Don was dealing with. Hypothermia was the largest concern, as temperatures at night were still dipping below freezing. Search and Rescue told us that after three days in current conditions, survival was not expected. Those pesky statistics were a faith drainer. But God had given His word. *Search until he is found!* And that's exactly what we were doing.

A small group of volunteers had arrived from the church to help us. I identified an area that had not been checked and sent them out on foot in a strategic search pattern. After searching for Don all day with two teams, there was still no sign of him.

Early morning on the seventh day, I was in the lobby near the SAR command center. "What time does the team start searching?" I asked. When Steven revealed that he was no longer looking for a live person, I knew we had to do something different. He was an ex-military bureaucrat who wanted control. He was locked into the statistics, but I was locked into what God had said. *Search until he is found!* Our much different goals were colliding.

I spoke cautiously, "What if we added another helicopter to the search? Of course, we'll pay for it and all associated costs."

"No, no, no, no, no!" Steven was clearly threatened by the suggestion. "Two helicopters in the same airspace are too dangerous—"

"Wait a minute," I interrupted. "I'm an airline pilot and instructor and FAA jet examiner. I own a jet charter company. I know a little bit about aviation. Listen, Steve, we can set grids to stay in different areas, out of each other's way. Aren't our chances of finding Don better if we have more people searching?"

"Absolutely not. No way. This is not going to happen," he barked.

"Look, I'm working for God, and I'm helping that woman over there as a volunteer." I pointed toward Virginia. "You're working for the State of Arizona. Your assignment is to search and rescue. Why don't you search according to your rules, and I'll search according to mine? I can search where you are not. Let's work in harmony with each other."

I had instructed Paula to charter a helicopter and pilot, stressing we needed a Jet Ranger. I knew that would be more expensive, but with high altitudes and strong winds in and around the canyon, for safety it needed to be jet powered. Having flown a Jet Ranger over New York City many times, I was familiar with its capabilities. I believed it offered the right balance of safety, power, maneuverability, and cost. I told Paula to have it meet us at a specific place on the canyon rim, where we could originate our own search.

Our company had some money in savings. We decided to use it all for the helicopter, to accomplish God's directive. I was already paying for several people's hotel and meals, but that wouldn't find Don. We needed more eyes in the air. And fast!

Paula wired several thousands of dollars to an aviation company in Las Vegas. Within a couple of hours, the helicopter touched down. Bill, the pilot, was young and eager, willing to do whatever I asked of him. He and I had instant accord. At almost the same time our chartered helicopter landed, the SAR chopper had broken down and was grounded, waiting for a new part that would take at least three days to arrive. The conflict over airspace no longer existed.

It was mid-morning of day seven. Our small group was optimistic and ready to search for Don. I asked Charlie to be in charge of the air search and told the pilot, Bill, to fly wherever Charlie directed as long as it was safe. "Charlie will know where the trails are, and he'll guide you. Remember, until he is found!"

Charlie had been there since the beginning and was familiar with the maps and what areas had already been checked. I would remain at the hotel where I could coordinate the ground and flight search teams, staying in communication through my aviation radios, newly purchased for the task.

We learned a lot from the Rangers—who are good at what they do. They traverse trails, going back and forth looking for clues. Specifically, they watch for clothing debris—usually the first sign of a lost hiker. When hikers become hypothermic, their bodies are dangerously cold, but they actually feel hot. This causes them to shed their clothing. Most of those who die in situations similar to Don's, are naked or nearly so when their bodies are found.

Faith in what God had promised kept us going. Our small team agreed that no one would speak about statistics, or finding only a body. Faith was needed to see the miraculous. Faith in God's promise would bring Don back home alive.

But a fight is a fight. The Bible talks about fighting the good fight of faith. I encouraged the others that we'd search, as our battle cry declared, until he is found—found alive according to our prayers.

The team prayed again. The helicopter took off while the others set out on foot. Three people were in the chopper. Bill flew, while Charlie and Mark searched out both sides of the chopper with binoculars. To maximize our efforts, I provided long-range radios for easy communication. Everyone on the team was feeling the pressure of time. No one rested or stopped to eat during daylight hours.

I stood at the canyon rim, 6,000 feet above the floor. The sheer magnitude made me feel like a bug in comparison as I watched the chopper grow smaller in the sky. It was easy to understand how someone on the trail below could become disoriented and lost. The main canyon branched into smaller canyons, weaving a maze of pathways easy to follow but leading to a dead end most of the time. Gaining perspective from the canyon floor was impossible. It was simply too massive. I whispered another prayer, "Thank You, Father in Heaven, for answering prayer. Thank You for bringing Don back alive."

I had visited the Grand Canyon a dozen times before, but always during the summer when the temperature commonly reaches 90 degrees, up to a high of 120. If you don't have enough water and shade, you can easily become dehydrated and disoriented. Those are the conditions that cause most deaths in the canyon. But this was early April. The winter snow was still on the ground, and nighttime temperatures dropped below freezing. Let's face it. This canyon is entirely unforgiving no matter what time of the year.

Inside the canyon, the helicopter looked like a gnat. It was barely visible as it followed the prescribed search pattern. I reviewed God's promise to Paula and me. The shepherd will leave the ninety-nine to search for the one sheep that is lost… and search until he is found! This was God's promise and for me, His directive.

God had given us His promise, but we had to respond by becoming His hands and feet, by taking action as an expression of our faith. We were all doing that by searching and speaking in faith. Keeping our faith strong was a constant battle of pushing out the doubt and fear and replacing it with God's Word.

The entire seventh day passed without so much as a trace of Don. *How can this be happening?* The disappointment was difficult to hide. Most of those who had come to help now needed to return to their responsibilities, leaving us with only four people and a helicopter. We felt gutted. That meant our search would be limited to the air—and there was only enough money to pay for one more day of flying.

Adding to our frustration, SAR decided to shut down their search. With their helicopter grounded and the statistical chances of finding Don alive nearly zero, they were wrapping things up and clearing out.

It was the morning of the eighth day, and we were searching entirely on our own. It certainly seemed illogical and even ridiculous that we were holding on to faith that we would find Don alive. The volunteer searchers who were now going home, shoulders sagging, were heartbroken. We could feel the ridicule from some on the SAR team.

A verse came to mind, as often happens when I'm struggling and contemplating what I should do.

> *I call Heaven and earth as witnesses today against you, that I have set before you life and death, blessing and cursing; therefore choose life, that both you and your descendants may live* (Deuteronomy 30:19).

It always comes down to a choice. Faith is a choice, and I had to choose once again. Each of us remaining had to choose. *Do I lead this small team and continue to believe the promise God gave? Or do I count our losses and let go in defeat?*

Using a chart and insights from those who had been searching on the ground and from the chopper flights, I guided them into an airborne search grid over a previously unscoured area. It felt as if we were all holding our collective breath. Every time the radio crackled, I grabbed it in anticipation. The hours ticked by. Once again, all day searching, searching, and more searching. But nothing was found—not a trace. At best, we had an hour of sunlight left.

The stress was showing in Virginia's deeply creased face and wringing hands. I could see the doubt and fear growing. It was easy to understand why.

Tension was building among the volunteers, too. Dusk now turned to darkness with no sign of Don. It was as if he had disappeared off the face of the earth.

Darkness finally brought a halt to the day's search. I called Bill on the radio. They had landed the chopper on the rim to contact me and ask what they should do. I analyzed how much flight time we had left before the money was gone. Maybe an hour. Two at the most. Just enough to fly back and land at the base. For all practical purposes, the search was over.

I bowed my head. "Lord? What do You want me to do? What shall I do now, Father?"

I believe in the power of God's Word. I've also learned how important individual faith is in our daily life. Jesus prayed for God's will to be done on earth as it is in Heaven. Following His will is different here on earth because of satan's resistance, but the principles don't change.

I thought of a Scripture in Mark 4. It teaches that, when God gives His word, satan comes immediately to steal it. It goes on to describe how persecution and tribulation come to choke out the word that was sown. This was the battle we were fighting, and we were certainly feeling the heat of it.

God had sown the promise in my heart. *Until he is found.* Now, circumstances were piling up to steal my faith and choke out that living word—to get me to relax my grip of faith. We were living in the moment of decision. Everything was on the line.

Night had fallen, and the chopper was out there in the blackness, parked somewhere on the rim of the vast Grand Canyon. And Don Johnson? There was no sign of him. His poor wife had finally given up and retreated to the privacy of her room.

Sitting in a chair in the hotel lobby, I heard that still small voice again. "What man of you, having a hundred sheep, if he has lost one of them, does not leave the ninety-nine in the open country and go after the one that is lost, until he finds it?" The shepherd found the lost sheep alive and brought it home, rejoicing. We would do the same.

I got on the radio and asked Charlie to arrange a joint communication between him, Bill, Mark, and me. My request surprised everyone. "Are you willing to stay there overnight so we can search a couple of hours in the morning?" Silence. Each person thought long about what I was asking. It was a lot. The nighttime temperatures were cold, and there was nowhere for them to lie down. They would all have to huddle up in the helicopter and wait nine hours for the sun to rise.

If everyone was willing to stay put until morning, we would have a couple more hours with the helicopter.

Pilot Bill got approval from his boss to stay another day by donating his salary. Then everyone agreed to spend the night sitting in place. I lay on the hotel lobby carpet with the radio by my side. We spent the night cold and uncomfortable—and praying. Even Bill was praying silently with us.

About 5:30 a.m., the radio crackled. "Dale? You copy?" It was Charlie. The temperatures had dropped into the teens. They were cold but ready to tackle this last search effort during daylight as the helicopter returned to base.

I gave them directions for the new, previously unchecked area. It was our last chance to find Don.

Just before takeoff, I led the team in prayer over our radios, "Father, in the name of Jesus, we once again thank You. You are always faithful and true to Your Word. Thank You for leading us to Don. Direct us to find Don alive, on this flight. Lead and direct, and provide funding for us until he is found! Thank You, Father. I pray this in the name of Jesus. Amen."

I've learned it is easiest to give up faith in the eleventh hour, as a sense of hopelessness grows. But sometimes I've observed God moving even after time has run out. I struggled to keep my mouth from speaking what appeared obvious to the others. All involved knew we were out of time and out of options—except for this last flight, which was actually a "return to base" operation. We'd look along the return flight path, a different route than we'd used before.

I gave last-minute instructions: "Bill, as before, you're in charge of the helicopter and the aviation part of the flight. Stay legal. Stay safe. And, Charlie, once again you're in charge of the search. Fly the route that we've agreed on—unless you are sure God is leading you otherwise.

"One last thing, gentlemen. Bring Don back. Alive. Find him and bring him back according to our prayers of faith. Do you understand? Do it God's way. Bring that chopper back with Don inside! Copy?"

"Copy. We copy all," Charlie responded. A click on the radio—and then silence. I was alone in the hotel lobby. I prayed in the Spirit. I praised the Lord for His faithfulness and His love, and for always answering prayer.

The helicopter lifted off and headed south, as agreed. Charlie gave me updates every few minutes. It was almost as if I were inside the aircraft with them. Proceeding farther away from base, they were planning to turn west, following the agreed flight path. Suddenly, Charlie said he sensed a tug on his heart that he interpreted as God's leading. He instructed Bill to turn east up the next canyon for just a peek into the small artery. Bill shouted over the sounds of the rotor blades. "We're low on fuel. I can do it for a minute, maybe two...but no more!"

They scoured the landscape with binoculars. No one spoke. Within seconds, Charlie yelled, "There! I see something!"

Bill turned the helicopter slightly so they could all see below. Strewn in the snow were a jacket, shirt, socks, and shoes. Clear signs of a hiker in the final stages of hypothermia.

I was startled by the crackle of the radio. "Dale. We see a naked man on a rock below. It's got to be Don. We think we've found him! You copy?"

"Copy!" I held my breath, waiting.

On a large rock, someone tried to stand, then collapsed back into a heap. The man lay motionless on top of the boulder. He rallied, trying to stand again, even lifting his arms. The men in the helicopter watched in disbelief as he fell off the rock into the snow. It had to be Don! And he was alive! But barely.

The helicopter touched down a short distance away from the boulder. Charlie and Mark jumped out, racing toward the frail man on the ground. Don was barely conscious. He'd been freezing without food or water for over a week, and could not stand. Don had always been tall and slim, but now he looked more like a bag of bones than a living person. Wrapping him in a blanket, they carried him back to the helicopter.

The radio crackled to life. "Dale! We've got him! Dale! It's Don, and he's alive! He's barely conscious, but we've got him! He's in the helicopter, and we're bringing him to base. Dale, you copy? He's alive!"

"I copy! I copy! Praise the good Lord! He's alive! Bring him here."

"Until he is found," I whispered. "Thank You, Father."

"This is chopper 5 Alpha Tango. We have Don Johnson onboard. He's alive! Headed back to base now."

To this day, I don't know how Don's wife heard the news, but she bolted into the lobby screaming, her face filled with anticipation. "What's happening? What's happening?" Tears streamed down her cheeks.

I grabbed her arm and told her the news. Moments later, we ran toward the spot where the helicopter would land. We could see it getting larger as the noise of the rotor grew louder. We held our breath as they touched down and the prop slowed to a stop.

Charlie and Mark opened the door as I raced forward and lifted Don's frail body out of the helicopter. Virginia ran toward us. Don was barely recognizable. Virginia gasped, then wrapped her arms around him, sobbing in relief.

Don was probably six feet four inches, and I don't think he weighed over a hundred pounds at that moment. We wrapped him in more blankets and gave him warm tea and soup. We started making calls. Summoning a doctor to the phone, we followed his instructions to transport Don to the local hospital immediately.

God had promised. In faith, we had agreed, and—the most difficult part—we had stayed and fought the "good fight of faith" to the end. The process had been so much harder than any of us had expected. But God had brought it to pass—His promise had been fulfilled through our faith in action. Praise the Lord! He is faithful!

The next day, we learned that Don's internal organs had already begun shutting down before he was rescued. The doctor said if he had not been found that day, he would not have been found alive.

I was home within twenty-four hours, jumping back into work—as busy as ever. A few days later, I looked up to see Paula walking into my office with a large, beautiful vase of flowers. Smiling and teary-eyed, she read the note accompanying the bouquet.

> Dear Dale, you saved my life! I am forever in debt to you. May God bless you and Paula always! —Don Johnson
>
> Thank you, Dale, for never giving up! *Until he is found!* —Virginia

CHAPTER 20

ADVENTURES IN SOUTH AFRICA

I say to you that likewise there will be more joy in heaven over one sinner who repents than over ninety-nine just persons who need no repentance.
—LUKE 15:7

As I advanced the throttles to full takeoff thrust, the Learjet raced down the runway, straddling the centerline until it leapt into the air. A joint sigh of relief was heard from pilots and passengers alike, as the city of Lusaka, Zambia, disappeared from sight.

A day and a half earlier, we had landed at Lusaka International Airport with an emergency. Although our flight plan had approved us to land there for refueling, once our jet came to a stop, we were surrounded by military at gunpoint and escorted to holding rooms, where we remained under armed guard.

While the traumatic ordeal unfolded, no one slept—but all prayed. Through our love and witnessing, God gave us the privilege of leading several of the soldiers to the Lord. In fact, my own copilot—a proclaimed athcist—also accepted Jesus during our internment. There's nothing like persecution to bring people to their knees. God had truly turned what satan meant for evil into good!

As the pilot-in-command, I received a brutal tongue-lashing from the military general in command of the airport. But after a process of diplomacy and prayer, we were finally released.

Set free and airborne, we rejoiced and praised the Lord. The weather was perfect for flying. Blue skies. No wind. I hadn't slept since departing Israel two days earlier and was exhausted. But with the estimation that we would be in Port Elizabeth, South Africa, by 4:00 p.m. local time, and the hope of a bed only a few hours away, my spirits lifted.

The primary passenger of this trip was Paul Crouch, founder and president of Trinity Broadcasting Christian TV Network (TBN). My company was managing the TBN aircraft, and I had been flying for him for almost two years without charge. It was my way of giving back to God. Whenever TBN needed to travel, I would captain the jet as the pilot-in-command and provide one of my company's flight instructors to accompany me as first officer.

Cruising at 40,000 feet, I turned and opened the cockpit door to communicate with the men in the cabin behind me. Most were dozing from a great sense of relief accompanied by extreme fatigue. The autopilot was engaged, so there wasn't much to distract me until a bare foot showed up on my lap!

My eyes followed the leg to discover that the foot belonged to Arthur Blessitt, the man known for carrying a cross around the world.

Arthur's life of evangelism had started when he was a young man and had been diagnosed with an embolism in his brain—inoperable and terminal. The doctors told him there was nothing they could do. He was going to die.

A leader of the Jesus Movement, Arthur had already given his life to the Lord. But then God asked him, "Why don't you serve Me the rest of your life?" He thought, *If I'm gonna die anyway, why don't I give the Lord whatever time I have left?* That was the beginning of an incredible journey.

Arthur began to share the good news about Jesus on the streets of Hollywood—passing out gospel tracts, answering questions, and praying with anyone who let him. Eventually, he began carrying a ten-foot wooden cross, which quickly caught the attention of passersby. Arthur became known as "the guy with the cross."

His ministry evolved into carrying the cross over 43,340 miles across 324 countries, including the full length of South America, Central America, and North America. He has led more people to the Lord than anyone can count, and his stories are diverse, spectacular, and miraculous.

Sitting in the cockpit at 40,000 feet, I asked with a smile, "Is there a reason your foot is on my lap, Arthur?"

He responded, "Feel the bottom of my foot." Steve, the first officer, and I exchanged a questioning glance as I felt the bottom of Arthur's foot.

"Do you feel any calluses?" he asked.

I shook my head in surprise. *How could that be?* Arthur had walked over nearly every continent and had no calluses. In fact, his foot felt smooth and soft.

He continued, "Smooth as a baby's bottom, right? What does the Bible say?"

His question piqued my curiosity. At this point, I turned to the copilot, "You've got the airplane."

I gave my full attention to Arthur as he quoted Romans 10:15: "How beautiful are the feet of those who preach the gospel of peace, who bring glad tidings of good things!" He continued, "I've been all over this world with those feet. How could they be so soft? And how about that embolism in my brain? It's never been operated on, never even been looked at again—and I'm still going, thirty years later."

We continued our conversation in low voices as the others slept. The aircraft hummed at cruise altitude, while the instrument panel gently illuminated the cockpit with its amber, green, and white lights.

"You've probably never been down here, right?" I pointed out the window at the Sahara Desert below us.

"Oh, yeah, Dale. I've been all over Africa."

"What?" I was shocked.

The land below was so vast, yet Arthur answered matter-of-factly, "Yeah, I've carried the cross from the tip of South Africa to the very top of the continent."

I stared at him in wonder and then at his foot, which he slipped back into his shoe. Then I asked him a simple, yet life-changing, question. "Arthur, how do you win people to the Lord? What's your technique…your secret?"

He laughed. "I don't have a technique! I just smile with the love of the Lord. Then I answer questions. That's all I do."

I was stunned. "That's your secret?"

"It's not a secret, Dale." Grinning, he left the cockpit and headed back to his seat. I shook my head, pondering Arthur's "technique" as we began our descent into Port Elizabeth.

After taxiing to a stop in front of an executive terminal, I helped the passengers unload their baggage and sent them off to the hotel with the first officer. I stayed behind to inspect the aircraft and make arrangements for minor maintenance as well as for the jet to be fueled and parked for a few days.

Once the airplane was secure, I unbuttoned a cowling on the nose section and removed a trash bag containing 1,500 gospel tracts. I had hidden them so they would not be confiscated in any of the Arab countries we traveled through. I always carried gospel tracts, giving them out all over the world at every opportunity.

Catching a taxi, I arrived at the hotel just before 10:00 p.m. I could hardly wait to get to my room and sleep. It had now been three days since I'd slept more than a few minutes at a time—and then usually sitting up.

Tossing my things on the bed, I reached for the phone to call Paula. I brought her up-to-date on our location and briefly recounted our harrowing experience in Zambia. Finishing that call after midnight, I fell on the bed and was instantly asleep.

Hours later, I was awakened by a command. "Dale, go!" I knew the voice. It was the Holy Spirit, whom I had learned to recognize and trust. Looking at the clock, I realized it was about six in the morning, but I felt surprisingly refreshed.

"Go where?" I asked aloud. My response was greeted with silence. But I knew what I had heard, so I climbed out of bed and dressed.

There were a lot of things I still didn't know about God. But His voice, I knew. When He said, "Dale, go!" I knew I should go, and He would tell me where when it was the right time for me to know.

Quickly putting on blue jeans, white athletic shoes, and a white T-shirt, I grabbed the 1,500 gospel tracts and my wallet, and headed downstairs to find out where I could rent a car. The man at the front desk smiled and said, "Right here. Where are you going?"

Shrugging my shoulders, I replied, "I don't know yet." I filled out the paperwork and paid the money. As I walked out the front entrance, the valet handed me the keys. It was then I realized the steering wheel was on the wrong side of the car—at least for me. I drove carefully away from the hotel, trying to adjust to driving on the "wrong" side, grateful it was early and there wasn't much traffic on the road.

I was ready to go, but where? A short distance down the road, I parked on the shoulder and prayed. "Where are You sending me, Lord? Where do You want me to go?"

I heard the still small voice say, "Go there."

Years before in Heaven, I had learned that communication was heart to heart, not through the ears and mind. Although I did hear sounds, music, and spoken words during my visit, most of the information I was given came directly into my heart—then from my heart, it would transfer to my mind.

Since returning from Heaven, sometimes when God speaks to me, my heart hears words. But the words always come with deeper and more complete understanding. That was happening now—an understanding of which way to go that came with words that seemed audible, but I knew they were not.

I turned onto the freeway on-ramp, heading north. "Okay, Lord, I'm Yours."

I did not argue or question what I was doing—I just responded with a desire for the Lord to lead me. I trusted Him. And I had learned to obey.

I followed the two-lane freeway, cutting through the sprawl-ing city for about twenty minutes before the surroundings changed to rural subdivisions. *Why hasn't the Lord told me any-thing else? Where is He taking me?* As I approached each exit, I asked, "Lord, do You want me to get off here?"

Silence.

I continued another thirty minutes as the landscape changed from scattered subdivisions to dirt fields dotted by an occasional house or farm.

As if He needed reminding, I prayed, "Lord, just tell me when and where to get off." There is no better place to be than follow-ing the Lord's direction, but I have to admit that it's unnerving when there seems to be no direction forthcoming.

Driving an unfamiliar car in a strange country on the left side of the road was a challenge. But driving by faith was even more so. Resisting the doubt and uncertainty that continually tried to creep in became an ongoing battle.

About an hour and a half northwest of the city, I finally felt prompted to turn off the highway. Eagerly, I began looking for the place the Lord was directing me to go. But there was noth-ing there—no buildings, no town, no sign to indicate where I was. Nothing. Just the highway and an off-ramp. Doubt flooded my mind.

Have I made a mistake? I turned left and kept driving. Soon I noticed a large grouping of rickety homes made of tin, card-board, and plywood. Nothing professionally built—only home-made shacks without trees, grass, or flowers. A narrow dirt road entered the small shanty town, but it was a road without any visible cars.

A short distance ahead, I spotted a small market of sorts. Pulling off, I parked and went in to find out where I was.

A musty smell greeted me as I walked through the rickety wooden door. The building had a concrete floor so chipped and worn it barely hinted of blue paint from long ago. Various colored ice chests lined the wall. I assumed they contained cooled items. The bulk of merchandise, consisting of snacks, basic food stock, and an assortment of household necessities, was crowded onto homebuilt wooden shelves.

The middle-aged owner, a tall, thin black man, seemed as surprised to see me as I was to be there. Grabbing a bottle of water from a shelf, I smiled as I approached the counter. "Is that a town over there?" I asked, motioning toward the small community. "Does it have a name?"

"No, that's a township. You can't go in there."

"Really? Why?"

"You can't go in there…it's illegal."

Surprised, I pressed him for further explanation. "What do you mean that it's illegal to go in there?"

He looked at me with concern. "You're white, and that's a black township. It's dangerous. Don't you watch the news?"

"No, I'm not from the area," I responded. He proceeded to recount a recent situation in which a white man had been beaten to death in a black township.

I thanked him for the water and information and headed back to the car. *This might be a good time to abort this possible misunderstanding with God. Maybe I was wrong to believe that God brought me here. How do I know for sure I heard from the Lord? How do I know?* I had felt as though I was supposed to take that off-ramp, but I hadn't heard an audible voice. *Maybe this new information from the shop owner is a warning.*

Who am I, anyway? What am I going to do if I walk into that township? Then I remembered what Arthur Blessitt had shared with me the previous evening in the cockpit. "I smile and answer questions." I felt that familiar prompting begin to witness to my spirit.

As I peered at the entrance to the township, my spirit started burning in my gut—and I knew. I knew God was sending me *there.* A Scripture popped into my mind: *"Have I not sent you to preach the gospel to the poor?"*

But I was just a pilot, not a professional minister. Still, I sensed that this was what God was telling me to do. I took a couple of sips of water, grabbed my bag of 1,500 gospel tracts from the car, and headed across the street.

Rejecting the fear and questions that were mounting with each step, I thanked the Lord for what He was going to accomplish and added a prayer for protection and guidance as I increased my speed.

Putting a smile on my face, I turned onto the dirt road entering the township. Almost immediately, two young adult males came running toward me. *They don't look happy that I'm here.* I smiled as they stopped right in front of me. They held no weapons. Although they looked stern, they did nothing threatening.

The older of the two asked, "Who are you, and what are you doing here?"

Ahh…there's my first question.

I imagined how God saw these two young men. He loved them, and right now He wanted to love them through me. That understanding made it natural to smile.

"My name is Dale Black. Sometimes people call me Captain Dale because I'm an airline pilot from America. I just arrived last night in a private Learjet, and I'm here today because God sent me to this place…to talk to you."

"To talk to us? About what?" one of the men asked.

There was my second question.

Still smiling, I answered, "I came here to talk about God and Heaven. Do you think you will go to Heaven when your life is over?"

The younger man looked at me suspiciously. "Do you know something?"

"I know God loves you. I believe He has asked me to ask you a question. When you die—and, of course, I hope that doesn't happen for a long time—but when it does, do you think you will go to Heaven?"

They looked at each other, confused. Turning back to me, the younger one replied, "Yeah, yeah, I think so."

"That's wonderful!" I responded. "But why do you think God would let you into Heaven?"

"Because my mother took us to church when we were growing up," he replied. "And we believe in God."

I reiterated, "Oh, okay. So you believe you're going to go to Heaven because you went to church and you believe in God?"

The older boy looked at me, somewhat frustrated, and muttered, "Yeah, I hope so."

"Well, that's good that you went to church," I replied. "And a lot of people believe that going to church gets us into Heaven." I opened my bag and took out two gospel tracts, handing one to each of the young men.

"This little booklet tells us what God says in the Bible about how we can get to Heaven. Isn't it true that we're all going to die someday?"

"Yeah," they responded in unison.

I continued, "Well, knowing where you'll go after you die is really important. Would you like to know what God says about how to be sure you'll go to Heaven? He's the expert, right?"

They both nodded.

"Well, the Bible says…" I continued reading through the small gospel tract, step by step, including the accompanying Scriptures, to explain clearly what God has said we must do to go to Heaven.

I read John 3:16 to the two boys: "'*For God so loved the world that He gave His only begotten Son, that whoever believes in Him will not perish but have everlasting life.*' You want to have everlasting life with God in Heaven, right?"

"Sure," they replied.

"Okay, well, it isn't about going to church. Although that's good, it's not going to get you to Heaven. The only way to get into Heaven is to have a right relationship with God. Sin separates us all from God. And the Bible says everyone has sinned, and the wage of sin is death. But God loves us so much that He solved the problem by sending His perfect Son, Jesus, who never sinned, to die in our place and pay the penalty for every person's sin. All we have to do is accept the free gift of salvation that Jesus offers."

They listened patiently and respectfully as we read through the gospel tract.

When we finished, I asked each of them if they believed what we had just read. I went on to ask if they would like to pray and ask

Jesus to forgive them of their sins and live in their hearts so they could have a relationship with God and go to Heaven someday.

They both nodded eagerly.

I held out my hands toward them. "Just grab my hand," I encouraged. "I'm going to pray for you. And if you agree with what I'm saying, just repeat the words after me."

The next thing I knew, they grabbed my hands and lowered their heads. I began to pray. "Father, please forgive me of my sins."

They softly repeated the words.

"I believe Jesus is Your Son, and He died in my place. I give my life to You. Thank You, Jesus, for saving me. Amen."

When the prayer was finished, they looked up, and they smiled for the first time since our encounter.

"Is that all we have to do to go to Heaven?" the younger one asked.

"If you meant what you prayed, then yes," I replied. "You know what this means? It means that you and I are now brothers because we're all in God's family."

"What?" the older one exclaimed, laughing. "He and I are already brothers," he said, pointing at the younger man.

"Well, I'm your brother now, too." I explained, "The Bible says that, when we accept Jesus as our Savior, we are adopted into God's family."

The older brother looked at me hopefully. "Could you come and meet our mother?" There was another question. *Wow! This sure is easier than I expected it to be.*

"I'd love to." Carrying my bag of gospel tracts, I accompanied them to a shack about ten houses down the dirt road. Hearing her sons call out, their mother emerged. A short, plump woman in her late forties, she stopped abruptly when she saw me. She looked confused. Glancing from me to her sons' smiling faces, her expression softened.

"Who are you? What are you doing here?" she asked. The conversation that followed was nearly the same as the one I had with her sons.

She told me that a missionary had introduced her to God when she was a young girl, and she had never forgotten that experience.

I asked her the same question I had asked her sons. Did she think she would go to Heaven when her life on earth ended?

"Oh, yes," she replied, smiling broadly. "I accepted Jesus into my heart when I was a little girl, and He's never left me."

"Perfect! The Bible says He will never leave us nor forsake us," I responded. "That means you and I are brother and sister. That's true, isn't it?"

"Yes, we are," she replied as she leaned toward me. "Did you share this information with my boys?"

The young men chimed in. "Yes, we prayed together. We're going to Heaven now for sure. And he's *our* brother, too." They chuckled again at the thought that we were somehow related.

Their mother's smile broadened. By this time, others had seen me in the community and were gathering around, wondering who I was and why this white man was there. Even though my skin is quite dark because of my partial Native American ancestry, I was still a "white man" here in South Africa.

As each new person arrived, I gave them a gospel tract. And after a time of answering questions and getting acquainted, I asked for everyone's attention. "May I ask you all a question?"

They all stopped and listened.

"Do you know for sure that when your life is over, you will go to Heaven?"

The group responded in a chorus of voices saying, "I hope so," or "I try to be good." Others said things like, "I go to church," or "I don't hurt anyone."

It was a fun and interesting conversation, and most were fascinated by the white man from America who had come to their small township to talk to them about God and Heaven.

I didn't have to think about what to say next or worry about it. I just followed the Holy Spirit's leading and answered questions. Most of those gathered prayed and asked Jesus to forgive them of sin and to come into their lives. It was glorious.

The mother asked, "Can you come across the road and talk to my friend? I've been praying for her for a long time."

"I'd love to," I responded with genuine delight. So the mother, her two sons, and I, headed across the street to the mother's friend's home. A group of about fifteen children and several adults followed along.

By the time the mother's friend came out, the gathering had grown to about twenty-five or thirty people. "This man has come from America," the mother announced, introducing me. "He's a pilot, and he's got an important question to ask all of us."

The friend looked at me expectantly. I began again. "Yes, my name is Dale, and the question God sent me here to ask you is this: 'If your life on earth ended today, do you think you would go to Heaven?'"

This woman I had just met scowled at my words. I handed out tracts to all who were present and took additional time to read through one of them aloud, revealing the plan of salvation in more detail. I explained the purpose of Jesus coming to earth. That He was sinless, and both God and man. How He laid His life down in our place, and why His shed blood paid for our sin. This precious woman drank in the words and softened toward me as I shared the good news.

I asked her the obvious question, "Would you like to pray and know for sure that you'll go to Heaven when your life ends?" I smiled at her as I held my hand out. After a brief hesitation, she took my hand and nodded. At that moment, I felt the mother's hand on my shoulder.

I looked around at all the faces surrounding us in front of this woman's home, so many precious people, watching and listening. I noticed the mother's joyful smile and her eyes filling with tears of emotion.

In a voice loud enough for all to hear, I said, "Anyone who would like to know for sure that their sins are forgiven and that they have a home in Heaven when this life is over, pray this prayer with me."

"Dear God," I began, and everybody repeated those words. "Forgive me, for I am a sinner. I believe Jesus is Your Son and died in my place to pay the penalty for my sins. Thank You, Lord, for shedding Your blood for my sins. I invite You into my heart and life, and I choose to live for You. Amen."

The woman tightened her grip on my hand as she prayed. At the end of our prayer, she looked up with tears running down her face and whispered, "I didn't know He loved me this much…to send someone from America to help me understand. Thank you."

The mother moved in to hug her dear friend, who was now also her sister in the Lord.

I was surprised by the spontaneous singing that erupted. The people were singing a familiar Christian song that missionaries had planted many years before. Almost everyone joined in, the children bounced with the melody, and others swayed in unison. It was a glorious picture of new believers praising God!

Hearing their praises took me right back to vivid memories of Heaven and the community of people who had met me there years before. Love, praise, and joy had radiated from them all. What a glorious memory I revisited as I looked around at all these smiling faces, full of love and joy, their hands lifted.

In Heaven, praise is as spontaneous and natural as breathing—quite different from the church I had been raised in, where most people simply held a hymnal and looked down with serious faces while they sang. This vision of people praising God with their voices and bodies was a natural reflection of Heaven. I drank in the images and the presence of God that inhabited their praise.

As the sun rose and the cool morning turned to a hot, dusty afternoon, I found myself on street after street lined with dozens of houses as people urged, "Come over here," or "There is someone you need to talk to." Every street looked like the last, and as we kept moving, I had no idea where I was. But news had spread throughout the neighborhood that an American pilot had arrived with a message from God. I spent the entire day in that little township, traversing the dirt roadways, smiling, passing out gospel tracts, and answering questions—invariably leading people to pray and receive Jesus.

I was repeatedly invited to stay for lunch, to have refreshments, and even to spend the night. I'd reply, "Thank you, but

I'm fine." I didn't need any food or drink. I was doing what I had come to do, what the Lord had sent me to do.

I remembered the Scripture where the disciples told Jesus, "Lord, You should eat something." But Jesus replied, "My food is to do the will of the Father." In that moment, I understood what Jesus meant. How refreshing it was to share the good news with these precious people. How satisfying it was to be used by God to reflect His love. During the entire day, I didn't need or even want food or water. I was entirely satisfied—more than satisfied. My heart was completely, joyously overwhelmed.

As the sun began to dip lower in the sky, I realized that all 1,500 of my gospel tracts had been handed out and I had walked every dusty street in that township. I looked down at my white tennis shoes, now brown with dirt and dust.

As I made my way back toward the entrance of the township, dozens of residents accompanied me, still smiling and singing as we said our goodbyes. They shouted invitations to return, thanked me for coming, and waved lovingly until I was across the street and back in my rental car. I thought of the man in the store whom satan had used to spark fear, and thanked the Lord He had helped me dismiss the enemy's threats and obey His leading.

As I drove away, watching the township become smaller in my rearview mirror, I shook my head in wonder at what God had just done. I started weeping, overcome with immense joy, knowing I would see again in Heaven someday, so many new brothers and sisters.

God had gone before me and with me. His presence was palpable. He had added over 700 to His family from that small township. I was simply an instrument, a spiritual midwife willing to participate in His plan.

My drive back toward the city was spent in overwhelming praise and thanksgiving. The joy I felt was more than I could contain as tears continued to roll down my cheeks.

Suddenly, the encounter with Arthur in the cockpit the night before, came flooding back to my mind. I realized that God had divinely orchestrated that encounter in preparation for what He had planned for today.

God had made it so easy for me—to simply smile and answer questions.

I've repeated what happened that day over and over throughout the years, in over sixty countries. I've learned the importance of waiting for the question and always being ready with the answer.

In the silence of the drive back, I again heard the unmistakable voice of God come into my heart. The voice was so strong I pulled to the side of the road and parked. He repeated His message: "Tell My people that it's harvest time—now!"

I am reminded of the words of Jesus in Luke 10:2 (AMP): *"The harvest is abundant [for there are many who need to hear the good news about salvation], but the workers [those available to proclaim the message of salvation] are few. Therefore, [prayerfully] ask the Lord of the harvest to send out workers into His harvest."*

This world is racing toward self-destruction. And Jesus has warned us that the time is coming when no one can work. As the dark grows darker, the light shines brighter for those who have eyes to see and ears to hear. There are millions who have never been more ready than they are today, to hear and respond to the gospel of Jesus Christ.

It *is* harvest time—now!

CHAPTER 21

TO RUSSIA WITH LOVE

And He said to them, "Go into all the world and preach the gospel to every creature."
—Mark 16:15

It was early 1990, and we were headed to Russia! The wall had just come down, allowing tourists into the former communist country. In addition, we were traveling to Israel. God had stirred the hearts of nineteen Christian laypeople to intercede and minister in these two ancient countries that will both play a role in end-time events.

Each team member had paid their own way and also contributed toward bringing thousands of Bibles and gospel tracts. We were gathering from across the US, plus one from Europe, to travel to Russia and then to Israel, to intercede over the countries and to pray for the people.

After spending about ten years leading ministry teams throughout the world, I had learned a few things. One goal was needed with every team, in every country, right at the beginning of every trip.

It was essential that the team be sequestered and trained for ministry by bringing them into one accord. The power and value of being in *"one accord"* is something I learned during my visit to Heaven. We see the power of it reflected in the Bible in Acts 2. I knew we needed to be a team of one mind and one spirit—in *"one accord"*—if we truly wanted God to use us according to His will and in powerful ways in Russia.

Growing up in the United States during the '50s and '60s meant that traveling to the USSR was almost never considered. I had always heard that the Russian people wanted world domination and that they were harsh, underhanded, and did not believe in God. Our team was in for a complete surprise.

Certainly, the Russian communist party was atheistic and diametrically opposed to Christianity. But then came Gorbachev, *Glasnost* (openness), and *Perestroika* (restructuring). The Berlin Wall had recently come down and everything was changing. For the first time since shortly after WWII, commercial flights were once again permitted into Moscow, the capital of the Russian Federation.

After three days of training and prayer, we departed San Diego, California, like a military unit—united and focused on what God had for us. The mission of this group was to pray effectively over the key places of government in Moscow, Russia, and throughout Israel—that the gospel message of Jesus Christ could be brought into these countries and shared with power.

The journey began with a non-stop flight to New York, then on to Stockholm, Sweden, where another person from Europe joined us. As a team, we prayed together and shared our personal testimonies of how God had worked in our lives, how He had orchestrated and divinely appointed bringing us together for this occasion.

Our goals were exciting ones: to pray for the country, share the gospel message of Jesus Christ with the people who were open, and make contact with Russian Jews wanting to return to Israel.

Our ministry owned and operated a Boeing 707 four-engine jet, donated to us by Kenneth Copeland Ministries. My wife, Paula and I, along with partners of the ministry, were donating funds toward an engine retrofit of the Boeing 707 and interior refurbishment, all in preparation for ministry work. One of our primary goals was to use the jet to transport Russian Jews to Israel.

It is interesting how our ministry team came primarily to pray for Russia and Israel, as well as make contact with Russian Jews. But God had other plans. Better plans. Plans according to Heaven's perspective more than ours.

Our Eagle International Ministry team would mark a historic moment in time, and be among the first arriving from a Western country in over 45 years.

We were filled with anticipation and excitement as our plane touched down in Moscow. Our airliner pulled up to a single-level terminal, where we disembarked down the stairs onto the tarmac before being directed into the terminal.

We'd been told it was now legal and politically acceptable to bring Bibles into the country. But had anyone told the Russian military? They were everywhere, carrying guns, making their presence quite intimidating. It was obvious that the more medals the soldiers wore on their jackets, the higher their ranking. And clearly, medals were important to the Russian military. But every one of them carried the unmistakable AK47 and a side pistol.

With a team of Americans now on the ground, nobody in Russia seemed to know for sure how the military would respond. In turn, we didn't know what to expect. In former years, entering Russia with Bibles certainly would have involved great risk, resulting in imprisonment for those caught under the regime of the former USSR.

In faith, we had brought a pallet of boxes carrying 9,000 Bibles in the Russian language and 200,000 gospel tracts. Because we were unsure of our reception, each team member also carried a dozen Bibles and a thousand gospel tracts within their personal luggage.

Rows of passengers crowded into a series of roped lines, anxiously waiting to get through immigration and clear customs under the watchful eyes of armed military.

We were enamored with the Russian people. In spite of their stoic façade, they seemed genuinely curious about the group of Americans who wouldn't stop smiling. This was a new and novel experience for everyone, and we all desired to interact.

MEETING SASHA, MY TOUR GUIDE

A slim man in his late 30s, dressed in a white shirt, dark tie, and jacket, approached our group. He was looking for Dale Black. He introduced himself as our assigned tour guide. There were no smiles. He was courteous but conducted himself in a strictly business-like manner.

I had the distinct impression that he was being watched, which would explain his behavior. But it was inconsequential to our mission and certainly didn't unnerve me. I knew that God was ultimately in control and would have His way in all that transpired.

Sasha was instructed to be "our guy." He would help us through customs, get us where we needed to be, and manage our time in Moscow from start to finish. He spoke perfect English, but with an unmistakable Russian accent. Sasha hovered like a mother hen to make sure we knew what was expected, but was a complete gentleman in the process.

As our team waited for our luggage, we spotted the boxes of Bibles and gospel tracts, which were stacked on a pallet, being rolled toward customs. I assumed they would be waiting for us on the other side of immigration.

Sasha and I continued to discuss the many details of what our time in Moscow would entail. He was as uncertain about where we could go as we were. The country was changing daily due to *Perestroika* and *Glasnost*.

I explained that our primary goal was not typical sightseeing, although we did want to visit certain areas. However, the reason for our trip was to pray for the people of Russia and to connect with the Jews who were desiring our intervention for immigration to Israel.

Sasha's expression reflected his surprise at such a strange plan, but he nodded in agreement. He informed me that this was the first time any foreign tour group was able to have access into previously unseen parts of the Kremlin—parts he himself had never seen.

We gathered our luggage and as a group followed Sasha toward customs. Suddenly, there was a commotion in the airport ahead. The many boxes of Bibles and gospel tracts, still on the dolly, had been surrounded by armed military and were being wrapped in plastic.

It appeared they were in the process of being confiscated. Just then a military soldier came up to Sasha and pointing at the boxes, speaking to him in Russian.

Sasha turned to me and communicated that the Bibles were not going to be allowed into the country. I looked directly into Sasha's eyes and spoke fervently. "No, Sasha! This is not possible! These Bibles are God's Word! They are gifts for the Russian people. We bought these as gifts at our personal expense. It's not propaganda. It is Almighty God's Holy Promises. These Bibles are *gifts* from American citizens for the Russian people. Sasha, listen, please. These are not small trinkets! These are precious gifts—eternal gifts—for the Russian people."

Sasha was stunned and unsure how to respond. I turned to the team who were all standing and staring at the pallet being wrapped. "People. Pray. *Now!*"

Like a military unit called to battle, the team members quickly surrounded the dolly and the military soldiers and began to take authority. With hands raised, they began praying out loud as they continued circling the boxes of Bible and gospel tracts. It was a sight to behold. The commotion captured the attention of all who were in the area. No doubt the audience in the terminal had never seen such a display.

Sasha was stunned. Trying to diffuse the situation quickly, he explained, "Dale, Bibles have not been allowed into Russia in my entire lifetime. It's not just you. It's anyone. Everyone. No one is permitted to bring Bibles into the Russian Federation. No one." His panic was growing. It was his job to direct and manage our group while we were in Russia. And this situation was clearly out of control from his perspective.

I tried to explain, "Our team paid for these Bibles personally, Sasha. In these books, you're going to find stories about Moses leading the children of Israel across the Red Sea. You'll find descriptions of Heaven. The birth and life of Jesus. You'll learn about miracles and about healing from God. Also, freedom from sin, eternal life, and a lot more." I was pointing toward the pallet of boxes as I spoke, imploring Sasha to help whoever was in charge to understand.

"Oh, Sasha. Please, sir, do whatever you can to change this situation, but we *must* have those Bibles and tracts."

There was a large Russian military man studying our group from across the terminal. As our eyes met, he turned immediately and walked away, disappearing into a back room. Within minutes, a mature soldier covered in medals emerged from the same doorway and walked slowly toward Sasha and me. It was clear that he was a man of authority. Sasha whispered toward me, "He's the general in charge."

He was the general of the Russian military overseeing the entire airport. Speaking to Sasha in a deep Russian voice, he did not even glance in my direction. They bantered back and forth. Sasha was trying urgently to explain how important the Bibles were to the Americans as they were personal gifts to Russian citizens.

The general had the last word and turned to walk away. Sasha slowly faced me, "I'm sorry, Dale. The Bibles will not be permitted. Nor the pamphlets. There is nothing more I can do. I'm sorry."

I can barely describe the feeling that came over me. It was like waves of electricity. Instantly, I knew God had a plan, and I responded without question. Quickly approaching the pallet where the general was speaking to the men wrapping the pallet, I stood firmly in front of him as Sasha scurried to keep up, unsure of what he had gotten into.

Looking directly into the general's eyes, I spoke. "If you are going to confiscate these Bibles, you are taking something more precious than gold. But if that is what you're going to do, please listen to me for a moment. We willingly give them to you, sir. These are our gifts to *you*." Sasha interpreted as I continued—his eyes growing wider.

"But before you take them away, could I please, *please* have just one?" I pled with the general, looking directly into his eyes. "Please, sir. Just one?" I knew the Holy Spirit was directing me. Our team had gathered just behind Sasha and me, and their prayers quietly continued. With dozens of curious and perplexed onlookers, I pleaded, "There is *one person* that I need to give *one* Bible to. I urge you to give me one Bible, sir. May I have just *one, please?*"

Sasha tried to interpret, uncertain how the general would respond. Soon the general turned toward a soldier, waving his arm and giving him abrupt instruction. A box was cut open and one Bible was removed and handed to me.

Everyone was standing and watching, wondering what was going to happen next. Turning back toward the general, I said, "Thank you so much, sir. Thank you. You see, God told me that there is one person that *must* have this Bible. His very *life* depends on it." Sasha tried to keep up, interpreting while bracing for whatever would come next.

Holding the Bible with both hands, I knew what God was telling me to do. "This Book is priceless. And God has someone very, very special He would like me to give this to. Thank you, general, for allowing me to do that." Holding the Bible tenderly, I thanked God for returning this one Bible to me.

It seemed that every person in the airport had stopped to watch the drama unfold. In many cases, this was a first experience with a group of Americans. I imagine they wondered if this was normal.

Then I extended the Bible toward the general and said, "God has told me to give this Bible to *you!* You, sir, are that person God wants me to give this Bible to."

Sasha looked at me in shock as he told the general what I said. The general appeared confused and embarrassed. But he quickly took the Bible out of my hands and tucked it into the front of his military jacket. Turning, he quickly marched past the pallet and disappeared into a back room without a word.

Sasha's eyes blinked rapidly in disbelief. He had never witnessed anything like this in his entire life. And he had only been our tour guide for 20 minutes!

We left the airport without Bibles or gospel tracts. But as a team, we prayed, claiming them for the Russian people and asking the Lord to bring them back into our possession.

Although our team had grown in love and unity since we first met in San Diego, I could tell that there were still some issues with egos and personalities that were not fully surrendered to the Lord. And so I suggested to one of the team members who was more spiritually mature, that we do some fasting. We asked for volunteers, encouraging those who were willing to join a fast. Several on the team agreed to participate, and things began to change by the next day.

My teenage son, who was traveling as part of the team, had brought his skateboard with him. At that time of his life, he and his skateboard were inseparable. And he was very good at riding it and performing most of the stunts that abound with skateboarders. Little did we know how invaluable that would be—an American teenager doing tricks on a skateboard in Moscow.

The activity drew an instant crowd of onlookers. He was given a Russian military hat by a soldier fascinated by the show, which he then wore most of the time. Our team went into action, talking to those in the crowd, handing out gospel tracts and sharing the gospel message of love.

On the second day in Russia, we were informed that all the Bibles and gospel tracts had been cleared through customs and were available for us to pick up at the First Baptist Church of Moscow. No one, not even the military or the tour guides, fully understood what was legal under the new guidelines. Everything was still changing so quickly.

Sasha was in awe that the Bibles had been returned and went with us to the Baptist church to pick them up. The pastor of the church invited us to sit in a special seating area in his church the next Sunday, which we planned to do. Leaving some of the gospel tracts with the church, we took the rest for our street evangelism outreach. Little did we know just how wondrously God would use those gospel tracts to bless the Russian people, and us.

During those first days in Moscow, we visited Red Square and the other major government buildings where we prayed and interceded for the Russian people and their country. Sasha took us to all the typical tourist places. And in each place, we prayed. Although Sasha had no idea why we did what we did, he respectfully began to anticipate our unorthodox ways.

By the third day, there was a significant breakthrough from our fasting. Our team was now bonded in the Spirit in a deeper, more humble way. No one tried to be noticed or to impress. We were all surrendered to the Lord's direction and His plan.

In the spirit of unity, we had made the decision as a group that each one would get to know everyone else on the team. So, every day, team members would sit on the bus or at a meal with someone they did not know well. Our team grew in Christian love, bonding to one another in faith. The love of God exuded through us individually and as a group as the distractions of personal ambition, ego, and potential personality conflicts simply melted away. The Holy Spirit had truly brought us into one accord.

Each person began to recognize that just like a puzzle displays a beautiful picture when all the pieces are in place, we were each a part of the picture God was creating for His purpose in Russia.

What I call "spiritual critical mass" occurs when a group is in one accord under the anointing of the Holy Spirit. The power of this can't be overstated. Just as described in the book of Acts, the disciples tarried in Jerusalem, prayed and fasted, worshipping the Lord in praise and song. They finally arrived in one accord, allowing the Holy Spirit to be Spirit to descend in strength and power.

When I was visiting Heaven, unity was as much a part of Heaven as God's holiness. Everyone there was in complete unity. It was so powerfully wonderful that I will never forget the feeling of that much love. Experiencing such perfect connection eliminates the need to have an ego. It erases the desire to find fault when there is such perfect love and we are so completely accepted. In Heaven, each difference is another reflection of

God's creativity, which is honored. On earth, differences provide another reason to misunderstand and divide.

What I experienced helped me better understand what happened in the Upper Room. When God's people put their individual desires and egos out of the way, allowing God's Spirit to preside, the Holy Spirit is then welcome to come in power and force—bringing God's attributes with Him. The disciples opened the door of Heaven by coming into agreement with Heaven and allowing God unrestricted access to their lives on earth.

Since my new understanding of the power of unity, I knew nothing was more important to accomplishing God's will on earth as a group, than that.

It is painful to see the lack of unity in the Body of Christ here on earth. It is a constant reminder that we are living in a fallen kingdom and God's people fall victim to it every day. It causes distrust, criticism, ego to rise up, all as self-protection. Safety is only found in God.

I had learned that God expresses Himself where there is unity. Our team was now experiencing that glorious presence, that equipped us to accomplish God's plan in power. We were ready.

The news around Moscow was that a McDonald's restaurant had just opened. On January 31, 1990, more than 5,000 people arrived at the opening day, to experience the famous McDonald's food. People stood in line for over 6 hours, and set a McDonald's world record of serving more than 30,000 visitors on opening day.

McDonald's meant very little to us. However, there was only one in all of Russia, and it was in Moscow. So we went to

McDonald's and saw a golden opportunity to love the people and share the good news of Jesus while they were stuck in line waiting.

People were lined up three or four abreast, and the line wound around the block, around the next block, across the street, and around the next block. The people had nothing to do but walk slowly as the line inched forward like a snail. We had a captive audience.

Separating into teams of two, we spread out along the line to share the good news. God's love, and the joy that was evident from His Spirit, created a magnetic attraction. Our team was instructed to do whatever God told them to do and say whatever God told them to say—God was clearly leading and directing.

Each team member had Bibles and gospel tracts to hand out. Americans in Russia were a unique and fascinating encounter for the people. And to be offered a gift was even more special. For the most part, all were eager to talk with us and wanted to ask us as many questions as we were asking them.

At each place in the line, we would try to find someone who spoke English and could interpret. If there was no one, our interpreter was summoned to help. All day long the gospel message was shared, using a gospel tract in Russian so people could read along.

We shared the timeless message—that everyone by faith can receive Jesus as their Savior, that He came to die in our place so that we never have to perish.

We quoted John 3:16-17 as evidence: *"For God so loved the world that he gave His only begotten Son that whoever believes in Him will not perish but have everlasting life. For God did not send his Son into the world to condemn the world but that the world through Him might be saved."* And so we would explain that Jesus is the answer to how to get to Heaven. And you can't get to Heaven without accepting the bridge between man and God—Jesus Christ.

At the conclusion of sharing what God has to say about how we get to Heaven, everyone was asked if they would like to know for sure that they would go to Heaven when their life on earth was over. It was an overwhelming response time and time again. For those who prayed and gave their lives to Jesus, trusting Him for the forgiveness of their sin, a Bible was presented that they could have as their own to further their spiritual growth.

We explained the message of salvation with joy and happiness. And the people, for the most part, received the gospel with joy. The team had been trained to love and share, not to debate, and it was working wonderfully. Based upon the number of Bibles that were passed out, I would guess that well over 400 precious people prayed to receive Jesus that first morning while standing in line at McDonald's.

In the afternoon, we went to a shopping area that attracted people who had more financial abundance and were generally more educated. Many were capable of speaking English, which allowed us to converse with larger numbers. We called it Rodeo Drive, as it reminded me of the street in Beverly Hills, California, that's lined with upscale, more expensive shops.

Repeating the same pattern as what we had done at McDonald's, we approached people in love and gave out gospel tracts. Then we asked the question. Praise the Lord, another 200 or so were added to the family of God and presented with a Bible to grow in their faith and understanding.

Everyone wanted to find out what the Americans were handing out and what they had to say. Most Russians had not had the opportunity to talk to an American until this point in time. We were among the first foreigners from the West to enter the country as tourists since the communist wall had come down. God had timed our trip perfectly.

There were a few people, usually the older ones, who already knew Jesus as Savior. These older Russians were finally able to speak freely about Jesus and their faith in God.

For 45 years, Christianity had been illegal. If you talked about Jesus, you could be arrested or imprisoned—and many were. Even to have a Bible in your possession in public had been enough to get you detained. And certainly, if you distributed any type of Christian literature, you would be arrested and thrown in prison.

God and communism are not compatible, and it was reflected in the lack of faith in the younger citizens who had never heard the gospel message and, therefore, did not believe in God. Churches consisted of only a handful of older people who had been alive prior to communism. But as we shared the gospel message, many from every age group received salvation.

For the first time in decades, this freedom to talk about Jesus, and give out gospel tracts to anyone who was open, was a rare and refreshing new era. People were eager to pray and receive a Bible. As we shared about having a personal relationship with God, it was fresh and new information. The Holy Spirit was clearly ministering to hearts wherever the gospel was preached.

Being instrumental in leading so many into a saving relationship with God through Jesus, was a thrill for our team members. Most had never experienced anything like it. I've said over the years, the fastest cure for depression is to tell someone about the love and saving grace of Jesus.

I've also said the biggest problem that exists in the world is that the majority of people don't truly understand who Jesus is. Nor what He has provided. I believe if anyone—anyone—gets a real understanding of what Jesus has done for them, they would want to serve Him.

There are so many precious stories and so many amazing miracles that took place during the ten days we were in Moscow. But there is simply not enough time to share them all. Over 100,000 gospel tracts were given out to individuals—always one on one. That's an average of each person on our team handing out over 500 gospel tracts every day.

Better still, is that a total of 9,000 Bibles were given to those who prayed to receive Jesus as Savior. All of that was accomplished through regular people who had left family and jobs for ten days, to serve the Lord with their time and ability.

Another 100,000 gospel tracts were left with the Moscow Baptist Church that had reached out to help us get the Bibles released from the airport. We forged a wonderful relationship with that church and its pastor.

Our ten days in Russia were a wonderful time of seed planting and soul winning. We were privileged to be laborers in the
eternal harvest of souls. Not only did we gain thousands of brothers and sisters, but we made many friends. We exchanged names
and addresses and stayed in contact with many for years.

We felt empowered and supercharged with love for God and
for His children. Each one of our team overflowed with the joy of
the Lord. And our mission was complete.

The night prior to our departure, Sasha, our Russian tour
guide, asked me if he could take me to a *very* special place. His
eyes were teary, and he spoke in a whisper, "Could you come to
my home and pray for me and my family? Just like you've been
praying for the people all over Moscow? Just you and me alone?
I really need you to pray for my wife and my son, too. Could you
do that, please?"

"Of course, Sasha. I'd be honored to meet your family and
pray for you," I responded.

After dropping the team off at Red Square for a last opportunity of ministry and prayer, Sasha and I boarded our small tour
bus, and he instructed the driver where to go.

Sasha seemed nervous and on edge as he leaned toward me
and whispered, "For my entire life, it has been illegal for anyone
besides my family to come into my house. KGB is especially
unfavorable for visitors from a foreign country. I don't know if
those laws have changed yet, but I could be in very much trouble
if anyone reports this."

Keeping one eye on the bus driver, Sasha finally alerted him,
"Park right here!" As the bus came to a stop, Sasha glanced down
the street in both directions, then pointing at a tall apartment

building a couple blocks away, he said, "You see that building? That's where I live. But you can't go in with me. I live on the fourth floor, apartment 421. This is what you need to do," he put his head down and spoke in low tones so the driver would not hear him giving me instructions. "Wait two minutes after I leave, then you leave. Don't look around and don't follow me. Walk confidently and go directly to the building next to mine. Take the stairs—not the elevator—to the sixth floor. There's a bridge between the two buildings that you can cross over to my building. Descend by stairway for two floors, and when you get to the fourth floor, turn to the right and approach my flat." He concluded by describing a secret knock I was to use. Then he left, and a few minutes later, I followed.

Soon, I was in his very small flat where he introduced me to his lovely wife and his little boy. I was the first visitor they had ever had in their home, and they treated me like royalty. Sasha showed me around as he told me about his life. They proudly showed me pictures on the wall of their families. That's when I learned that her parents, who were not present at that moment, also lived with them in the small apartment. My mind questioned how they could all live in such a small space. I was reminded of how blessed we are in America.

"Sasha, you asked me here to pray for you and your family. I will absolutely do that, sir. But first there's a question I'd like to ask you. Do you know for sure that, if you died today, you would go to Heaven?" I turned to his wife and asked the same thing again, as Sasha translated. Both shook their heads no, as they looked into my face. They had been raised atheist, and their exposure to Christianity was what Sasha had observed in the last ten days with our team.

But Sasha had been watching all week as thousands of Russian people came to know Jesus as Savior. He had been impacted by the joy and love he had observed. Each night, he had been sharing what he had seen with his wife. And he wanted what we were offering.

I explained the glorious message of salvation once again, while Sasha translated for his wife and son. Then I asked them if they would like to be forgiven of sin and commit their hearts to Jesus Christ as their Lord and Savior. They nodded yes, as they wholeheartedly agreed.

We held hands and I prayed as they repeated. They followed the prayer word for word in Russian, with their son repeating the words as he held on to Sasha's leg with both arms. I rejoiced as this precious family came into a saving knowledge of Jesus as their Savior and Lord.

There were hugs and tears and smiling faces. I shared with them that they had not joined a denomination or a religion but that they had become part of God's family through their relationship with Jesus Christ. That their spirit—the real person they are—had been born again. And from that day forward, they would have the Spirit of Jesus living in them to help and guide them into truth, and to empower them to live for Him. I told them that, because they were born again, when their life on this earth is over, they will go to Heaven and live with God and His family forever.

The family of God consists of hundreds of millions of people from all nationalities, all different languages. Yet it is one family, God's children bound together by the blood of Jesus. There is no other way to Heaven or to God, except through accepting Jesus as His only Son, and asking Him to forgive your sins and to live His life in you..

I quickly flashed back to the family I had met in Heaven years earlier. They were sent to greet me and welcome me to Heaven. Yet they were different colors and from different countries. Something I didn't even notice then. All I saw was the love each had for me and the joy they expressed to welcome me home.

Turning to Sasha, I smiled and said, "This makes you and me brothers, you know." Then looking into his wife's eyes, "And you are my sister. I am your brother. And there are hundreds of millions that are in this family. You are part of something wonderful."

I talked to them about what the Bible says about the importance of baptism and suggested that they get baptized by the pastor of the Baptist Church, the pastor who had helped us. They agreed, and those arrangements were made and handled in a wonderful way.

We then shared a glorious conversation, and I answered their questions about their new life in Christ. The change in their spirits was already clear to see. The joy on their faces and the love that exuded from them were precious reminders of the power of the new birth, through the work of the Holy Spirit. I am continually in awe seeing the fruits of the Holy Spirit's work when He gives a new believer a new spiritual heart.

I knew we had accomplished what the Lord intended and what Sasha had so desired. We hugged, said our joyous goodbyes, and I reversed my steps until I arrived back at the bus.

Sasha and I had been together for ten days. We'd done hundreds of things together and spoken countless times. He had been warm and kind—a complete gentleman and very professional since we had met. But now he was different.

For the first time, Sasha was so happy, he was actually giddy. He seemed overjoyed to belong to something bigger than anything he had ever dreamed of. I knew that he still had little idea of all God had for him. But he did understand that he was going to Heaven when his life on earth ended. He told me privately that he had a clean feeling—like heavy weights had come off his shoulders.

As we talked about what had occurred when he and his family prayed, and how precious that was, I explained to Sasha the importance of confessing Jesus as the Lord of his life to others. And then I told him of the Scripture where Jesus said, *"Therefore whoever confesses Me before men, him I will also confess before My Father who is in Heaven"* (Matthew 10:32).

I could tell Sasha was contemplating my words. As the team members boarded the bus and took their seats, recounting testimonies of what God had done in Red Square, it was a time of rejoicing. As things calmed back down, Sasha looked at me and nodded that he was ready. Standing, I got the team's attention, "Brothers and sisters, some of the greatest news is about to be shared. The angels are rejoicing in Heaven. Sasha, go ahead."

I invited Sasha to stand before the group as he had done dozens of times already in the last ten days as our guide. But this time it was very different.

Sasha, who had been so professional, lost his composure. He was simply not familiar with the emotions he was feeling as a reborn Christian. But he pressed through and shared that he had prayed to receive Jesus as his Savior and his Lord, along with his wife and son. Now Heaven was his home, and Jesus was the Lord of his life. Trying to control his emotions, he stressed that he and his family were now also part of the family of God.

When it was all over, Sasha was beaming. One of the team members started singing a chorus by Bill and Gloria Gaither called, "I'm So Glad I'm a Part of the Family of God." As the team sang, several came up and hugged Sasha, welcoming him into the family.

The Bible has a lot to say about Heaven. Sometimes we need to look more closely at the multifaceted aspects of God and His Word.

> But as it is written, "Eye hath not seen, nor ear heard, nor have entered into the heart of man the things which God has prepared for those who love Him" (1 Corinthians 2:9).

For me, it doesn't get much better on earth than to experience the *one accord* that comes from total surrender to the Lord Jesus Christ and the fellowship that is possible among those in the family of God.

Two hours later, we were on our way back to the airport where our adventure began. Our spiritual family had grown by the thousands while in Russia, and now our dear friend Sasha, was included in that number.

Our team boarded our flight, soon lifting into the air. All our eyes were fixed on the city of Moscow becoming smaller in the windows, as each of us revisited memories that were now indelibly imprinted on our hearts. I knew instantly that God was pleased with what had occurred. He was pleased because we had allowed Him to be strong in our weakness. We had surrendered to Him, and the harvest truly was plenteous. He had accomplished a mighty work, and it had been through our willingness to faithfully follow.

Upon arrival back home, we began at once to assemble a second team to return to Russia and Israel. That story is equally remarkable and a blessing to recount.

EPILOGUE

After I shared my journey to Heaven with my grandfather, he suggested that, instead of talking about it, I should *live* my life in a way that reflected my sacred experience. He said, "Live what you believe you *saw*. Live what you believe you *heard* and *learned*."

After much prayer, I determined that I would not talk about my heavenly experience but would live my life as a reflection of Heaven and all that I had learned. I sure tried anyway. I succeeded in not talking about my visit to Heaven for forty years. Not with anyone—not even members of my own family—until God made it abundantly clear that He wanted me to start sharing my story. First, I told my wife. As I talked, she started writing notes, which later became part of the book *Flight to Heaven* (Bethany House, 2010).

Now that you've read *Visiting Heaven*, you may find my experience believable, or you may not. That is your prerogative. You may recall that my primary purpose for writing this book was to help you gain a clearer understanding of God. Not only that, but hopefully you have learned more about how to connect with the God who created you and loves you.

This author is fully convinced that Heaven *is* real, and the God of the Bible is what this earth-life is truly all about. That leads me to ask, why not prepare for Heaven *now*? And while living on earth in the meantime, why not live with greater purpose each day? I often say that a life with Jesus Christ at the controls is *the* only way to fly.

Of course, you are free *not* to believe my story. But you may have at least surmised that something miraculous took place—something that changed me on the inside. You have the freedom to choose whether to believe or not to believe. Even God does not force you to believe in His Son, Jesus, the Messiah. Relationship with God and eternity in Heaven are yours to choose—or not.

Consider this. If your heart has been stirred by some of what you've read, would you at least be willing to learn more about Jesus? Someone once said that Jesus is either the biggest liar and lunatic that has ever walked the earth or He truly is the Son of God. And if He *is* the Messiah, then, according to the Bible, He is the *only* way to have eternal life with God in Heaven. Jesus is the bridge between earth and Heaven.

You are free to choose what you'll do with the information in *Visiting Heaven*. After all, it's *your* life. You are the only one who can ultimately decide where you will spend eternity. My assignment from God was to tell my story in the most accurate and easy to understand method possible. What you decide to do with what you've read is entirely up to you.

God created humankind in His own image. You are a spirit, you have a soul, and you currently live in a body. Both your spirit and soul (your mind, will, and emotions) are eternal and will live forever—with God, or separated from God for eternity.

The love of God is what changed me the most. I've come to understand that all of us were created to *want* to be loved. If we were completely honest with ourselves, I think we'd find that we were also created to *give* love, as well as to receive it.

And when we give of ourselves, a wonderful godly principle kicks into action. As we give—anything, whatever it is—we get it back. It's just one of the sowing and reaping principles of God and how He created things to work. Jesus said, *"Give, and it will be given to you"* (Luke 6:38). Whenever you give (or sow) something in faith, you get (or reap) that same thing back—multiplied!

This works in all aspects of life, including when you give your life to Jesus Christ. If you truly give Him control, He will give you back *new* life with *power,* with *purpose,* and with *joy.* The best part of all, is you also receive eternal life with God in Heaven when your life on earth ends.

Since the crash and my visit to Heaven, my entire purpose for living has changed. Life is short. It's also unpredictable. This leads me to bring up the most important question anyone can ask themself in this life, "Where will I go when I die?"

My greatest desire is that you would know the same loving God whom I have come to know. He loves you and has a wonderful plan for your life.

THE WORDS OF JESUS

Do your own due diligence and make the best discovery of all. Who is Jesus? Get a red-letter edition of the Bible, not a paraphrase. Personally, I use the oldest version I can get of the New King James Bible.

Read *everything* that Jesus said. His words will be written in red letters. Just read what He said. But when you read, keep your mind *alert* and your heart *open*. Ask God to speak to your heart and reveal what is true. Then fasten your seat belt!

If you'll accept my challenge sincerely, you may be shocked at what happens. You may soon realize that God's Word is living. It is also supernatural. And it is empowered by God's Holy Spirit to help you. His promises are for you, for today.

Once you've read for yourself about who Jesus is and why He came to earth, you'll be well on your way. Then make your own decision about what you believe and the place Jesus will have in your life.

It's *your eternal life,* so do with it whatever you will. But don't just believe what someone else tells you about Jesus. Don't believe just any preacher. And certainly don't believe the media or what others "say" about Jesus either. Take a few hours of your life to read the *real* words of Jesus for yourself. Then *you* decide. If you'll do that, I can promise you something. It will be the most important few hours of your life!

If after doing the above, you'd like to know how you can start a *new life* with Christ, go to Appendix B. There you'll find easy to follow steps to help you ask Jesus into your life and, to make sure you're going to Heaven when your life on earth is through.

> For whoever desires to save his life will lose it, but whoever loses his life for My sake will find it. For what profit is it to a man if he gains the whole world, and loses his own soul? (Matthew 16:25-26).

Below are current photos of the Portal of the Folded Wings monument. Installed on the wall inside is a memorial plaque reflecting the life God gave me. For over fifty years, I was told that no plaques could ever be placed above Amelia Earhart's inscription. But as you can see, *"with God nothing will be impossible"* (Luke 1:37).

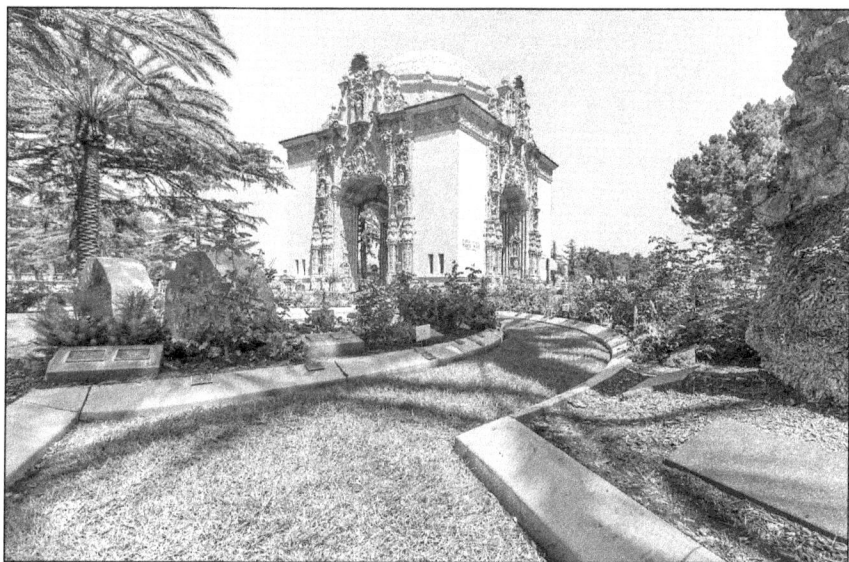

Portal of the Folded Wings monument at Valhalla Memorial Cemetery

Capt. Dale Black

January 1, 1950 -

The only survivor of aviation's most ironic airplane crash.
On July 18, 1969 Navajo N9150Y crashed into this mausoleum
"Portal of the Folded Wings"

Dale miraculously survived but with massive injuries. With faith in God
and enormous effort, Dale's life and career were incredibly restored.
He then dedicated his life to God and his career to aviation safety.

Airline Pilot: Golden West Airlines & Trans World Airlines.
Founder/CEO: American Eagle Aviation, Jet Flight International,
Eagle International Ministries.

Instructor/Standards Captain: Boeing 707, B727, B737, B747,
L-1011, numerous corporate jets and general aviation aircraft.

FAA Flight Examiner: Boeing 737, Learjet, Citation, ATP Certificate.

Recipient: FAA Wright Brother's Master Pilot Award -
Honoring 50 years of aviation safety.
Trained thousands of pilots in a career spanning five decades.

Jesus said, "I am the resurrection, and the life: he that believeth in Me, though he were dead,
yet shall he live: And whosoever lives and believes in Me shall never die." John 11:25-26
Do you believe?

Astounding true story is recorded in bestselling book:
"Flight to Heaven"

(Photo of plaques provided by Capt. Mike Guymon)

APPENDIX A

EYE EXERCISES

This method of eye exercise has worked well for me throughout a forty-year career as a professional pilot and beyond.

Several key ingredients go with the eye exercises. Faith in God, prayer, scriptural confession of God's healing promises, and a good diet that helps promote the body's natural immune system are all important.

To put it in simple terms: as the steward of my body, I worked to bring it back into agreement with God's original design.

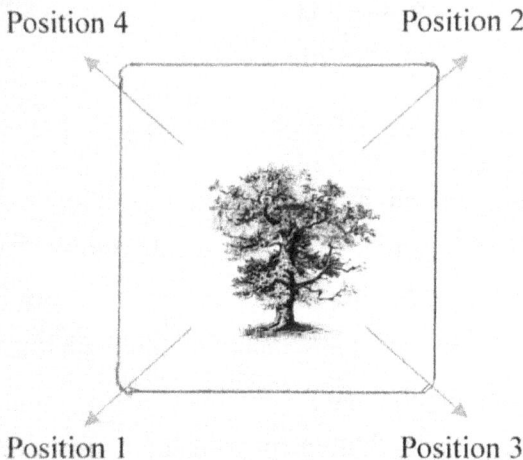

Illustration for Eye Exercise by Dale Black

INSTRUCTIONS FOR EXERCISE

Stand or sit with your body facing toward a window you can easily see out of. (Or you may prefer to sit or stand outside.) If you are wearing corrective lenses or contacts, remove them for these exercises.

Relax your body. Without moving your head, visually select an object in the far distance. Move only your eyes, not your head.

Focus on a detail of the object—like a tree branch or a leaf or the top of the tree. Or you can select an object on a building, like a piece of décor, or a house lantern, or doorknob. Or something like a transformer on an electrical tower. But select something in the far distance that you can see but with some difficulty because of the distance. Try to find an object that is one hundred yards away, or farther if possible.

Step 1

Focus on the detail of the distant object. It does not matter whether you can see it clearly. You probably can't—that is why you are using this exercise. Try to gain clarity as you hold your focus on the object for about five to ten seconds.

Step 2

Now, look at the tip of your nose and try to focus on that. If that is too difficult, put your hand about two to four inches in front of your face and focus on a detail on your hand, like a palm line or a freckle. Repeat this process of far/near for about five to ten seconds of focus in each position.

This will be a little bit uncomfortable for your eyes but should not be painful. Remember, you are working a muscle that has been largely unexercised.

Step 3

Holding your head stationary and continuing to face straight forward, move your eyes to your lower left-hand corner, as far down to the left corner as possible (i.e. position 1) for two to three seconds. This portion of the exercises does not require you to focus on a specific object. Instead, this will stretch your eye muscles—but *not* to the point of pain.

Then look toward your top right corner (i.e. position 2) for two to three seconds. Remember to move your eyes without moving your head. You're moving your eyes diagonally, bottom left to upper right, from lower left to top right. Repeat this three times—bottom left to upper right.

Step 4

Once again, look straight ahead at your distant object and focus again on a detail, holding your focus for five to ten seconds. Then look back at the tip of your nose or your hand in front of your face, focusing for another five to ten seconds.

Step 5

Holding your head straight forward and moving only your eyes, look to the lower right corner (i.e. depicted in position 3) and hold for two to three seconds, then to the upper left corner (i.e. depicted in position 4) for two to three seconds. Repeat looking to the lower right then to top left, for a total of three times each.

You'll feel the results of your eye muscles working out as you continue these exercises for several cycles. I recommend that you do them three times each day. It should take only about five minutes each time, and you should experience new results within a few days.

While you do these exercises, or before or after, be sure to thank the Lord aloud for giving you healthy eyes with good vision. Speak in faith, thanking Him for creating your eyes perfectly, and for the improvement you are experiencing through your stewardship of exercise. Quote some healing Scriptures like the one below, thanking the Lord for His Word. And then speaking aloud, give those Scriptures authority to reign over your physical body and specifically over your eyes and vision.

Remember Romans 10:17: *"So then faith comes by hearing, and hearing by the word of God."* This is why speaking God's Word aloud is so important. As you confess God's Word, and your ears hear God's Word, your faith will grow. Your physical body is an instrument of spiritual growth. When used correctly, your body will respond amazingly to what is happening in the spiritual realm.

If doing these exercises causes pain in your eyes, then do them less frequently or for a shorter duration, or don't stretch so far in each corner of the four positions. But keep doing them. Over time, your tolerance should increase just as a bicep would grow stronger and less painful by working it out over time.

While doing the eye exercises, make sure you're breathing deeply to help you remain relaxed and to add oxygen to your lungs and bloodstream. Also, be sure to drink plenty of water before you begin, and continue to do so throughout the day. Your eye muscles need oxygen and water to help them function at their best.

Remember that water is H_2O—two parts hydrogen and one part oxygen. Your body is made up of 75 percent water, and your brain is 85 percent. We need water! We lose water throughout the day through perspiration, breathing, and evaporation. It has been proven that most people are chronically dehydrated, and this one condition can compromise our health. It is highly likely that you need more water than you are getting in your body every day.

Do you wonder how much water you should drink daily? A basic rule of thumb is this: Calculate two-thirds of your body weight. Drink that many ounces daily. Example: a 150-pound person needs two/thirds of that weight in ounces of water. On a calculator, insert 150 x .67 to get 100.5 or approximately one hundred ounces of water per day. Other health experts commonly recommend 8 eight-ounce glasses, which equals about two liters, or half a gallon, a day. This is called the 8×8 rule and is very easy to remember. This is the minimum amount you should drink daily.

Be absolutely certain your water is adequately purified through a good water filtration system. Tap water is usually dangerous and contains fluoride and other harmful contaminates.

Do these exercises work? Oh, praise the Lord, they sure worked well for me. They helped me become a professional airline pilot and pass my annual FAA eye exams.

If I stop the exercises, my vision gradually deteriorates and I experience difficulty focusing on items near and far. Throughout my entire adult life, these exercises, along with walking in faith with God's healing promises, have helped me maintain my eyesight at a quality level without any correction.

You may not have previously known that your eyes use muscles to focus. Strengthening those muscles helps your eyes with their ability to focus. Sadly, the eye doctor doesn't recommend exercise but instead prescribes lenses that bridge the gap between your current poor vision and acceptable vision.

Without exercise, you'll find that your eyes become weaker over time, requiring a new and stronger prescription periodically. Why? Because the prescription makes your eyes work less; therefore, your eyes become even weaker.

God asked me to be responsible, and work diligently to be a good steward of my body. And He honored my efforts and responded miraculously to my prayers of faith.

God's ways are not the world's ways (see Isaiah 55:8-9). Yet I see most Christians run to the world's system first when they are in physical need. God can use doctors for good, but only in submission to His authority. We must first seek God and His righteousness.

When we are in need, God should be our first stop. And as we stay at His feet and ask Him what we should do next, He will direct us safely to the additional support we need.

The medical system has become more corrupt every year and often works in a way that is contrary to the will of God. Goals of the practitioners sometimes conflict with the overall goals of the patient. Patients usually want to get well, but medical protocols treat their symptoms rather than the root cause of the problem. This keeps the money flowing, people employed, and patients coming back again and again. Healing is not possible unless we deal with the root cause of the sickness or weakness rather than simply treating symptoms.

My wife, Paula, witnesses this regularly in her Winning Over Cancer Ministry. God works through both the miraculous and the practical to bring healing. In our fallen world, I see best results when individuals combine both the natural and the supernatural simultaneously.

The injury to my eye was a catalyst to life-altering change. Thankfully, I learned dozens of valuable heavenly keys to victory through that challenge.

No matter what happens in life, you can start over.

For there is hope for a tree, if it is cut down, that it will sprout again, and that its tender shoots will not cease. Though its root may grow old in the earth, and its stump may die in the ground, yet at the scent of water it will bud and bring forth branches like a plant (Job 14:7-9).

DISCOVER HEAVEN FOR YOURSELF

You can be *100 percent* certain that you *will* go to Heaven when your life is finished here on earth. You can have real and lasting peace right now through a relationship with Jesus Christ! Here's a simple way to start your journey to a new life with Christ.

STEP 1. KNOW THAT GOD LOVES YOU AND HAS A PLAN FOR YOUR LIFE.

The Bible says, "*God so loved the world that He gave His one and only Son* [Jesus Christ], *that whoever believes in Him shall not perish, but have eternal life*" (John 3:16).

Jesus said, "*I have come that they may have life, and that they may have it more abundantly*"—a complete life full of purpose (John 10:10).

So why doesn't everyone have this abundant life that Jesus talked about? It's because there's a problem.

STEP 2. MAN IS SINFUL AND SEPARATED FROM GOD.

We have all done, thought, or said bad things, right? This is called "sin." The Bible says, "*All have sinned and fall short of the glory of God*" (Romans 3:23).

But there is more. The result of sin is death, spiritual separation from God (see Romans 6:23).

Thankfully, there is good news!

STEP 3. GOD SENT HIS SON TO DIE IN YOUR PLACE—FOR YOUR SINS!

Jesus died in our place so that we could have a relationship with God and be in right standing with Him forever.

> *God demonstrates His own love toward us, in that while we were yet sinners, Christ died for us* (Romans 5:8).

But it didn't end with His death on the cross. He rose again and is alive today!

> *Christ died for our sins…He was buried…He rose again the third day, according to the Scriptures* (1 Corinthians 15:3-4).

Jesus is the only way to a relationship with God now, while you are alive on earth. And Jesus is the only way to get into Heaven when your life on earth is over.

Jesus said, *"I am the way, and the truth, and the life. No one comes to the Father except through Me"* (John 14:6).

STEP 4. WOULD YOU LIKE TO RECEIVE GOD'S FORGIVENESS?

We can't earn salvation. We can't be good enough to deserve Heaven. We are saved by God's grace when we have faith in His Son, Jesus Christ.

Here is what to do now: Accept the fact that you are a sinner, that Christ died for your sins, and then ask for His forgiveness.

Next, turn from your sins—that's called repentance. Jesus Christ knows you and loves you. What matters to Him is the attitude of your heart, your honesty.

Let me suggest praying the following prayer to accept Jesus Christ as your Lord and Savior. Don't wait, do it right now:

Dear Lord Jesus, I know that I've sinned, and I ask for Your forgiveness. I believe that You died for my sins and rose from the dead. I turn away from my sins and invite You to come into my heart. I give you the controls of my life. From this moment on, I plan on following You as my Lord and Savior. Amen.

If you prayed that prayer, and meant it with your heart, congratulations. You are a part of God's wonderful family. That means we are in the same family, and I am now your spiritual brother. If you prayed that prayer and meant it with your heart, you are going to Heaven, and I am so very glad for you. I'd love to meet you personally, if not on this earth, then for sure in our heavenly home provided to us through Jesus.

See you there.

To watch a short video called "Discovering Heaven," go to my website at DaleBlack.org

AFTERWORD

BY PAULA BLACK

N ow that you've read Dale's account of the airplane crash, his visit to Heaven, and a sampling of the adventures of faith that reveal a changed life, I would like to contribute a few words in closing. I've lived with Dale for over fifty years, and I can confidently confirm that his life was inarguably altered by his experience. Not once has he done or said anything, or made any directional choice, that did not reflect the reality of his experience in Heaven or his unshakable faith in knowing God.

In the early years, Dale would talk about how the crash changed him. I would say, "A lot of people have accidents, but it doesn't change them the way you've been changed." Throughout the years I would often ask him questions like, "Did you leave your body?" "You saw Heaven, didn't you?" I knew he must have had a profound spiritual encounter, based upon his life's actions. The only thing that would make sense of everything I witnessed about his life, is that he had visited Heaven.

Years later, we came to a major crossroad in our lives. That's when Dale finally told me the whole story. Right after his journey to Heaven, he had promised God he wouldn't share it with anyone until God clearly instructed him to. After forty years, God led him to share it with me.

Once I learned the whole story, I understood entirely why he was so changed. So many things made sense for the first time. Just hearing about his experience, also changed my understanding of life on earth, Heaven, death, and even God.

I grew up as a preacher's kid. My dad was a pastor in small-town churches and always needed a second or third job to keep food on the table and pay the bills. Throughout those years, I met many missionaries who spoke at our churches, and they were always just as poor and needy as we were. The ministry lifestyle seemed like too much of a struggle. I knew that was not the life I had *any* interest in. One thing I determined as a teenage girl—I'd never marry a preacher or a missionary.

Dale and I first met at college a little over a year after his accident. He made a big impression. He was the first young man I had met who seemed to love God more than anything or anyone else—yet he was not religious about it. I thought he was the most attractive guy on campus because of his genuine heart.

Dale's body still had signs of his many injuries, and he had some problems walking. He was also skinny after being in a wheelchair and then on crutches for so long. But what most impressed me, was his amazing heart. We would sit and talk for hours about everything. We talked about God and spiritual things, and even now, I can scarcely believe how special it was.

One day, he told me in no uncertain terms that he was going to become an airline pilot. His sheer conviction surprised me. I had never met anyone with such steadfast faith. This was before I learned the reasons for his faith.

I tried not to discourage him, but given the obvious obstacles, there was nothing in the natural to indicate he would ever succeed at such a lofty goal. Besides his physical obstacles, he had lost much of his memory—including how to fly airplanes. He would have to learn to fly all over again.

Still in the process of overcoming many injuries, Dale didn't seem to recognize how those challenges could possibly keep him from reaching his dreams. I had never met a person with such clear, unwavering belief and expectation. How could anyone know God that well? Could I have that kind of faith…that God's Word is absolute and immovable?

To make a long story short, we fell in love and got married, and I was incorporated into Dale's large family and his life of faith. He had already spent the previous summer on the mission field, wanting to give something back to God for all God had done for him.

A couple of months following our wedding, the two of us headed back to Peru to to donate our time and efforts on the mission field once again. Dale spoke fluent Spanish, so he was able to share the gospel of Jesus Christ in many places throughout Peru. Then we spent the summer preaching in the jungle villages of the Aguaruna Indians—an incredibly primitive tribe of people in the Amazon of northern Peru. This was quite challenging, given that the indians hunted with blowguns, never had electricity, and didn't understand what the shining silver birds, we call airplanes were, that flew far overhead. That missionary journey began our life of volunteer ministry that continues to this day.

In this book, you read about Dale hearing "the voice" in the cockpit. That was the first of many communications from God asking Dale to surrender.

Dale had become become familiar with receiving from God and having his prayers answered. He received healings and understanding, as his body was miraculously restored, against all medical or natural odds, following his massive injuries from the crash. He rejoiced at the fulfillment of his dream to be strong enough to fly for a major US airline…and so much more. I also became accustomed to receiving from God as I believed for these things with Dale. It was an exciting time in our lives.

After Dale surrendered his vocation with the airlines—a decision I fully agreed with—we were left with virtually nothing. No income and no clear plan. So Dale went back to driving trucks, and we started a small business in our garage, where he began training pilots. These were meager beginnings, and we worked harder than I had ever thought anyone could. We never borrowed money, always remaining debt free, and we tithed on every dollar.

I am now going to tell you something that will likely surprise you. At first, it may sound as though I'm bragging, but I'm not… read on. God had some unexpected course changes for us.

Within a few years, we had a booming and successful business worth more than twelve million in today's dollars. Our growing aviation company trained pilots to fly jets, like the Cessna Citation and Learjet. We also conducted aircraft sales and had a charter company that flew celebrities, CEOs, and the wealthy. We managed a fleet of corporate jets and other aircraft, including some we personally owned.

By this time, we owned several homes, drove luxury cars, had a business limousine complete with a full-time chauffeur, and enjoyed a live-in cook and maid. We were blessed to have a sizeable amount of cash in the bank besides, and enjoyed traveling with our children. Our life had become far more than I had ever dreamed possible. Certainly, we worked hard, but God had clearly blessed our efforts.

During this same time, we launched a Christian ministry and began using the aircraft we managed, and our funds, in gospel outreach—taking teams of lay people, food, clothing, gospel tracts, and the *Jesus* film—to over fifty countries. We saw tens of thousands pray to receive Jesus. Countless people from all over the world were miraculously saved and healed. Many miracles of every type occurred while we were out on the front lines of ministry. It was truly glorious.

During the height of our prosperity and business success, something shocking happened. The company limo was headed to the Hollywood-Burbank airport to pick up Dale after he returned from Berlin, Germany. I decided to ride along and surprise him.

The moment I saw Dale, I could tell something was brewing. His face was tight with apparent stress. Things weren't normal. Then he explained what he was sensing from the Lord. I knew God must have spoken to him on his trip and was not surprised—as that was not particularly unusual.

What I didn't expect was for him to tell me something that would change…everything.

What he told me God had said was a surprise: "Total surrender. Total obedience. Total dependence." I was shocked when he described that God wanted us to surrender our business, our possessions—our everything—and depend entirely on the Lord. It was obvious that Dale was nervous about how I would receive this extreme message.

I admit I was shocked—but not for the reasons expected. God had been pounding my heart for weeks with the same message—a full and complete surrender of all our earthly possessions.

Dale and I talked for days and prayed diligently. God was asking a lot. But we both knew it was true. We were being challenged to let go of the things we had accumulated and fully trust the Lord for our needs.

It wasn't an easy decision. On the other hand, it actually *was* easy. God had asked. Who were we to say *no*? He had given us so much and blessed us beyond measure. Nothing in this world is worth more than a surrendered and obedient relationship with God. We knew Heaven is real. We knew this earthly life is temporary. We knew that, when we said *yes* to Jesus as Lord, He would call the shots. We knew it would always be for our good. What we had to learn was that it would not always be easy. In fact, it would prove to be incredibly difficult.

We sold or gave away all we had. It took almost an entire year. With the funds, we built an orphanage in Guatemala, and a medical clinic in Peru. We funded the building of churches in various places where we had previously ministered.

People thought we were crazy. Dale's dad thought Dale had "lost it." Some wondered if we had joined a weird religious cult.

We learned the hard way, that many of our friends were not interested in continuing a relationship when we didn't have money or earthly trappings. God pruned us. He pruned us deeply and taught us how to trust in Him more fully. What powerful lessons we learned—most often in the valley of great difficulty—eternal lessons that are too valuable to put a price on.

The Lord taught us truths that helped us overcome terminal cancer a few years later. He taught us lessons that prepared us for the difficult last days—the days we are living in now. God helped us sever our reliance on, or our love for, the world.

In the Bible, we find Jesus telling His disciples how to live a righteous life and what it looks like to follow Him.

> *The young man said to Him, "All these things I have kept from my youth. What do I still lack?" Jesus said to him, "If you want to be perfect, go, sell what you have and give to the poor, and you will have treasure in heaven; and come, follow Me"* (Matthew 19:20–21).

My take on this Scripture is that, because the man was rich, he relied on his possessions for security. It appears he lived a godly life and believed Jesus was the Messiah but likely did not know the loss he faced by holding on to his earthly riches. The lack of trust in God that can occur when we have "more than enough" can rob us of eternal blessings. I am not saying it robs us of Heaven, but of the fuller blessing God would like to give us.

I'm also not saying that everyone reading these words should do as we did. I am saying, however, to listen to God's voice and do as He instructs. He wants only good things for His children—even if the process is difficult. But know that He looks at your life from an eternal perspective, not a worldly, temporary one.

> *Do not love the world or the things in the world. If anyone loves the world, the love of the Father is not in*

him. For all that is in the world—the lust of the flesh, the lust of the eyes, and the pride of life—is not of the Father but is of the world. And the world is passing away, and the lust of it; but he who does the will of God abides forever (1 John 2:15–17).

What's in store for Dale and me now? We believe we're living in the last of the last days before Jesus returns. Our assignment seems to be to help prepare those with hearing ears and pliable hearts, to hear the voice of the Lord and to walk in His ways. We have faith in His Word—His precious promises, that glorious victory is ahead—both during the process and at the end.

If reading this book has inspired you—stirred your heart—I'd like to challenge you to renew your commitment to Jesus Christ today. Fully surrender your life and future to His will. Be filled with His Holy Spirit. Make God's Word the final authority in your life. And allow Him to lead.

If you do that, you are ready to begin your own *adventures of faith.*

ABOUT THE AUTHOR

CAPT. DALE BLACK is a former airline pilot who has dedicated his career to professional pilot training, aviation safety, and missionary aviation. He has flown for over 40 years with 18,000+ hours of experience in a variety of commercial jets, as well as many corporate jets and general aviation aircraft. Dale is a former FAA Boeing 737 and ATP Flight Examiner, Safety Consultant, Accident Prevention Counselor, and a recipient of the Wright Brothers Master Pilot Award.

Dale has a BA degree from Point Loma Nazarene University. He has an earned MA in Theology and a PhD in Business. He was founder and CEO of a jet pilot training and jet aircraft sales company near Hollywood-Burbank, CA. For more than 30 years, Dale was a jet aircraft manager, and personal flight instructor, for executives and celebrities.

Dale married his college sweetheart, Paula, and they have two grown children. When Paula was diagnosed with terminal cancer and given 3 to 6 months to live, Dale turned his aviation accident research skills toward uncovering the root causes of cancer. As a result, and with God's healing power, Paula permanently reversed the cancer without chemo, radiation, or drugs. That was over 25 years ago. Her inspirational story is written in her book, *Life, Cancer and God.*

Eventually, Dale sensed God's leading to sell his multimillion-dollar business and their homes, to become fully dependent on God's provision. They sold, or gave away, all earthly possessions to follow the call that Dale describes as "total surrender… total obedience…total dependence." With those funds they founded an orphanage, built churches and medical clinics, and have led hundreds of teams around the world distributing Bibles and medical aid and spreading the gospel of Jesus Christ. Up until the printing of this book, Dale and Paula have given back every dollar of salary and all book royalties to further the gospel message of Jesus Christ.

OTHER BOOKS BY DALE BLACK

LIFE, CANCER AND GOD *by Paula Black and Dale Black*

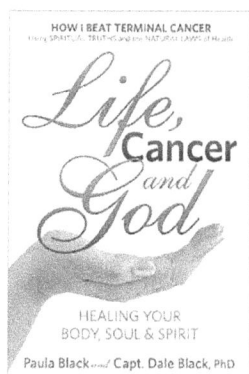

This book is the essential guide to beating cancer. Riveting! Shocking! Eye-opening. A roadmap to successfully treating all types of cancer.

As featured on the cover of *Publishers Weekly,* this beautifully written, inspirational, and enlightening memoir may be the ultimate victory-over-cancer story.

In the prime of life, as a wife, mother, and businesswoman, Paula heard the dreaded words: "It's cancer." Doctors diagnosed her with aggressive terminal cancer, giving her only 3 to 6 months to live.

She and her husband, Dale, began researching everything they could about her fatal disease. In the book, Dale and Paula describe their journey from advanced-stage cancer to complete recovery and vibrant health. This faith-based story is destined to be one you'll read more than once and want to share with others.

Prepare to laugh, cry, hold your breath, and shout for joy as you accompany this husband and wife on their incredible journey of faith, where personal struggles interact with biblical insight. Learn how Paula defied medical logic, cured terminal cancer permanently, and got her life back.

Statistics from the American Cancer Society state that 1 in 2 Men, 1 in 3 women, will get cancer in their lifetime. Reading this book could save your life.

RHONDA MCCUE
RN and Hospice Nurse

FORGET EVERYTHING YOU THOUGHT YOU KNEW ABOUT CANCER! The author's approach is startling—the "missing link" for those dealing with cancer, heart disease, diabetes, leukemia, and other chronic illnesses. Every person, sick or well, should read this book!

DR. ROBERT W. CHRISTENSEN
Maxillofacial Surgeon and Author

FLIGHT TO HEAVEN, *Capt. Dale Black*, *Bethany House, 2010*

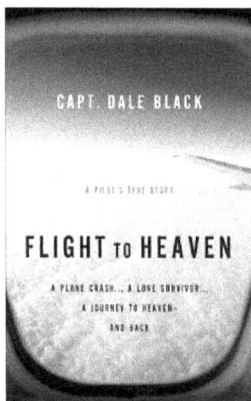

A pilot's true story. A plane crash…
A lone survivor…
A journey to heaven and back.

Capt. Dale Black has flown as a commercial pilot all over the world, but one flight changed his life forever—an amazing journey to Heaven and back. Hold on to your seat as you experience the heart-stopping flight over Zambia to the officially declared "non-survivable" airplane crash.

Hovering between life and death for three days, Dale experienced a wondrous journey to Heaven that will astound you. Against all odds, Dale miraculously survived, then contrary to medical prognosis, miraculously recovered from life-threatening injuries to fulfill his dream to fly again.

This "life after death" true story is both a page-turner and a faith-builder. The author does not commercialize his experience of Heaven but tells it in a humble and reverent way while using breathtaking descriptions. I have recommended this book to my entire church.

PASTOR KENNETH CETTON
Park Terrace Baptist Church

I purchased this book as a gift for my dad, a retired airline captain, but soon discovered I couldn't put it down. Both of us are professional pilots and we easily rate it 5 stars. The aviation aspects of the book are professional and technically accurate, yet the emphasis throughout is on a loving God. We think the book is a masterpiece and could be enjoyed by everyone, pilot or not.

CAPT. E. LAYTON
Boeing 757, Major Airline Pilot

HOW GOD HEALS
Dale Black (audio book, 3-CD Set)

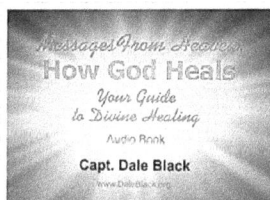

Your biblical guide to divine health. Learn how you can know with certainty that God wants you well. Find out why some are healed, and others are not. Does God use sickness to teach us spiritual lessons? Does God receive glory through our suffering? If healing is God's will, why aren't more people healed? Learn the answers to these and other tough questions while increasing your faith for healing.

THE *REAL NEAR DEATH EXPERIENC.* *STORIES* SERIES

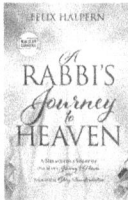

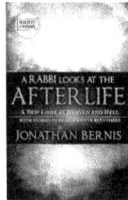